THE **CAT**
SELECTOR

First edition for North America published in 2011 by Barron's Educational Series, Inc.

All inquiries should be addressed to:
Barron's Educational Series, Inc.
250 Wireless Blvd.
Hauppauge NY, 11788
www.barronseduc.com

ISBN-13: 978-0-7641-6424-8
Library of Congress Control Number: 2010939396

Conceived, designed, and produced by
Marshall Editions
The Old Brewery
6 Blundell Street
London N7 9BH
www.marshalleditions.com

Managing Editor Miranda Smith
Project Editor Emily Collins
Production Nikki Ingram
Editorial and Design by Fairley & Booker

Color separation by Modern Age Repro House Ltd.,
Hong Kong
Printed in China by 1010 Printing International Ltd.

9 8 7 6 5 4 3 2 1

THE CAT SELECTOR

HOW TO CHOOSE THE RIGHT CAT FOR YOU

David Alderton

BARRON'S

Contents

Introduction

Although ordinary domestic cats are still kept widely as pets, many people are now choosing purebred cats as companions. A number of these breeds have a history that extends back centuries, as typified by the Siamese and Siberian. They originate from different areas around the world, with geography and climate having played a significant part in shaping their appearance.

Both the requirements and temperament of purebred cats vary widely, from one breed to another. So if you are attracted to having a cat of this type, there are a number of factors to bear in mind, to make sure that you choose not just a breed that you like, but one that is compatible with your lifestyle.

Perhaps the most obvious consideration relates to their grooming needs. Some, such as the Persian Longhair, require far more care in this respect than others. There is also a marked variance in size between different purebred cats. The Maine Coon ranks as one of the largest breeds today, as reflected by its appetite, making these cats more expensive to keep. Temperament is also varied, with certain breeds proving surprisingly vocal and lively, whereas others are much quieter and more relaxed.

This book provides a detailed visual breakdown of cats of all types—not just purebred individuals, but equally, some of the colors and patterns that can be found in ordinary cats. You can also discover not just well-established breeds in the following pages, but newcomers including the Kinkalow, some of which have almost certainly not featured in any book before.

Ginger

How to Use This Book

This book, with its comprehensive coverage of established and newer breeds, will help you to find your ideal feline companion. It will also allow you to discover more about the stunning range of breeds, colors, and patterns that now exist in the domestic cat, and to find out more about them.

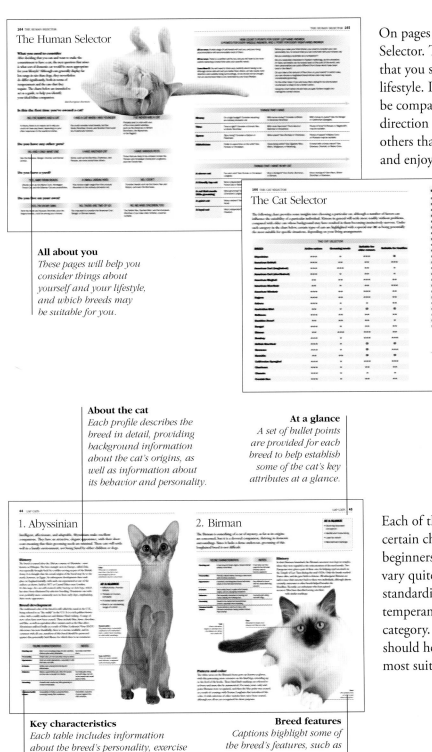

All about you
These pages will help you consider things about yourself and your lifestyle, and which breeds may be suitable for you.

On pages 164–167 there are two charts, The Human Selector and The Cat Selector. These quick-reference charts allow you to determine the types of cats that you should be considering, having carried out an assessment of your own lifestyle. It is so important to be sure that the cat you ultimately choose will be compatible in this regard. This initial selection will help steer you in the direction of individual breeds that are likely possibilities, while eliminating others that will not be suitable. Alternatively, just browse the main chapters and enjoy finding out about the cats that interest you the most.

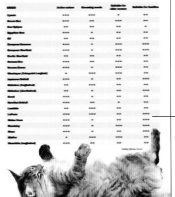

All about cats
This chart lists all the cats featured in this book in alphabetical order and provides a checklist for certain factors that may help you make your decision.

About the cat
Each profile describes the breed in detail, providing background information about the cat's origins, as well as information about its behavior and personality.

At a glance
A set of bullet points are provided for each breed to help establish some of the cat's key attributes at a glance.

Each of the main chapters of this book features ten breeds that have certain characteristics in common, such as cats that are suitable for beginners or those with particular talents. The cats included sometimes vary quite widely—for example, in size—but the information here is standardized, allowing you to directly compare the individual needs, temperaments, and appearances of the particular cats within each category. These pages, along with the charts at the back of the book, should help you reach a final decision as to which type of cat will be most suited to your lifestyle.

Key characteristics
Each table includes information about the breed's personality, exercise requirements, and other characteristics.

Breed features
Captions highlight some of the breed's features, such as coat color and body shape.

Dilute Torbie and White

Brown Tabby

Chinchilla

Choosing a Cat

Choosing a cat is not something to be rushed, especially as, with luck, you should be obtaining a pet that will be part of your daily life for the next 15 to 20 years—that is if you start with a kitten. There are a number of different factors that will influence your choice of cat, some of which will relate to your lifestyle, and others that will be a matter of personal preference, such as the type of cat that you are seeking. You need to consider whether you might want a purebred or nonpedigree cat, for example, and whether you would prefer a kitten or an older, house-trained cat.

Your choices in this regard will influence how you set about finding a suitable companion, and how to settle your pet into its new surroundings at home with you. This provides a great opportunity to build a close bond between you and your cat. Ideally, try to schedule this when you will be at home for most of the time, perhaps when you are on vacation. Bear in mind that successful introductions do require time and patience, even though cats, and kittens especially, can prove to be quite adaptable, living alongside not just people but dogs as well.

Golden Chinchilla

Preparing for a New Kitten

Obtaining a kitten can be expensive—and not just in terms of acquiring an individual. You will need food and water bowls (stable containers that are easy to clean), a food mat, a cat litter tray, a bag of litter, a scoop, and special disinfectant for cleaning the tray. You will also need combs and brushes, which will be influenced by whether or not your cat is longhaired, plus a cat crate for moving your pet.

Early days

Settling a young kitten into your home is not difficult, but avoid changing its diet for the first couple of weeks, so as to minimize any risk of digestive upset. Fresh drinking water must always be available, too. Kittens are instinctively clean, and the likelihood is that your new pet will already be using a litter tray readily. If not, though, start by placing the litter tray nearby soon after a meal, when your kitten is most likely to want to relieve itself.

Be prepared to change the layout of your home, so as to ensure that everything will be safe for your pet. Remove any valuable items that could be knocked over, as kittens can jump up on to furniture, and be sure to restrict your pet from the kitchen.

Health matters

Do not overlook the cost of essential vaccinations and deworming treatments, which are available from your veterinarian. There are several factors to bear in mind when it comes to choosing a veterinarian. You may have had good experiences of a local veterinarian before, or other animal-owning friends might be able to give you a recommendation. The veterinarian's location is an important consideration—ideally, it should be close to your home, so that you can seek advice easily.

Do not forget to investigate pet insurance as well, as this can bring considerable piece of mind. Young cats can easily end up being injured in accidents, and the costs of delicate orthopedic surgery can be very high. Nevertheless, compare different policies first and check that the offer is suited to your needs.

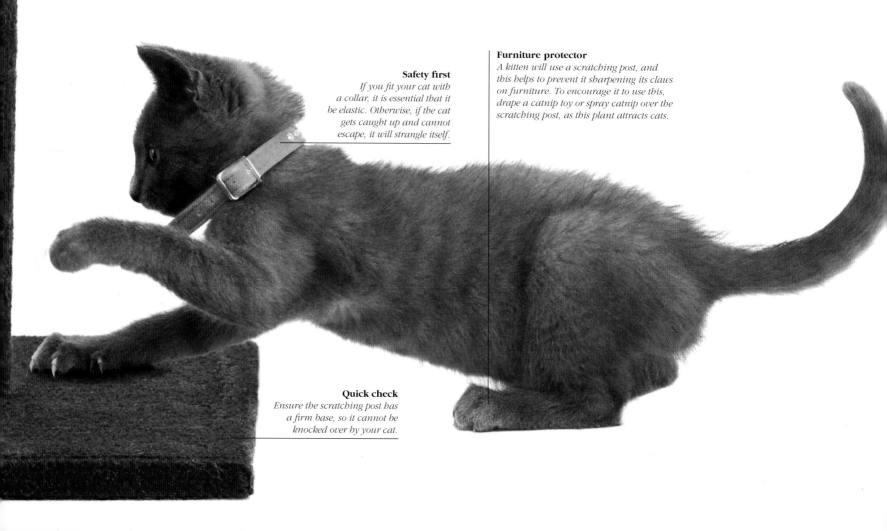

Safety first
If you fit your cat with a collar, it is essential that it be elastic. Otherwise, if the cat gets caught up and cannot escape, it will strangle itself.

Furniture protector
A kitten will use a scratching post, and this helps to prevent it sharpening its claws on furniture. To encourage it to use this, drape a catnip toy or spray catnip over the scratching post, as this plant attracts cats.

Quick check
Ensure the scratching post has a firm base, so it cannot be knocked over by your cat.

Cats outdoors

You must also decide if it is fair to keep your cat indoors on a permanent basis as it grows older, should you live in an apartment or adjacent to a busy road. If so, you need to be prepared to adapt your home, so as to accommodate your new companion, adding a play area for your pet. In cases where it will be relatively safe to allow your kitten to venture out of the home after it has completed its vaccinations, then fitting a cat flap is recommended. There are various designs on the market, and it is important to try to ensure as far as possible that the cat flap will not allow other cats from the neighborhood into your home. Aside from possibly fighting with your pet, they may also steal its food and even soil around your home.

Sepia Lynx Point

Health
If you are keeping two cats, choose littermates if possible. This is safer from a health perspective than introducing two from different sources.

Ginger and White

Food
Avoid sudden dietary changes with a new cat of any age.

Microchips

Chip-operated cat flaps function off a chip on the cat's collar. The most sophisticated designs will open automatically by reading the information contained in your pet's microchip implant, which is vital for identification purposes in any event. The microchip, which is about the size of a grain of rice, is effectively injected under the cat's skin at the back of the neck. This can be done in either kittens or older cats, and subsequently, if your pet strays and is handed into a rescue organization, it can be scanned with a reader that detects the unique code on the microchip. By referring to a central database, it will be possible to contact you, so you can be reunited with your pet.

Cost
Two kittens will settle well together in a new home, but bear in mind the extra costs entailed in keeping a pair of cats rather than just one.

Chocolate Birman Crossbreed

Choosing Your Cat

Having evaluated the impact and cost of owning a cat as far as your lifestyle is concerned, the next stage is to think about what type of cat appeals to you and would be most suitable. The number of recognized cat breeds has grown significantly over the past decade to more than 80 in total, and there can be very distinctive behavioral differences among them.

Black British Shorthair

Choosing a breed

If you want a fairly placid cat that should live happily indoors, then a Persian (see page 73) could be suitable, or alternatively, at the other extreme, one of the so-called "hairless" breeds, of which the Sphynx (see page 149) is still the best-known example. They will leave relatively little hair around the home, making housework much easier.

Other family members may affect your decision, too. Should you have relatively young children, then a tolerant breed such as the Ragdoll (see page 50) can be recommended. If you are seeking a breed that is likely to live in relative harmony with a dog, then an Abyssinian (see page 44) is often a good choice. Allergies to cats are not unknown—if this might be a possibility, then picking one of the hairless breeds or a Russian (see page 98) might be less likely to result in an adverse reaction.

There are also circumstances where some breeds may not be an ideal choice. Should you enjoy attracting birds to your yard, for example, then cats that are eager hunters, such as Siamese (see page 86) and Orientals (see page 63), are probably not recommended. A breed that displays almost no hunting instinct is the Ragdoll.

Blue British Shorthair

Black-and-white Persian

Nonpedigree cats

In spite of the surging number of new cat breeds, the vast majority of pet cats are still simply derived from ordinary street-cat stock not belonging to any breed. Many people prefer such cats, highlighting their even temperament and adaptability. They are not noisy and demonstrative like the Siamese or quiet like the Russian. Even in the case of longhaired nonpedigrees, their coats are unlikely to be as profuse as that of a Himalayan (see page 70), for example, and so their coat care is easier.

Another point that attracts owners to nonpedigrees is the fact that they are quite individual cats in terms of their coat patterning. Whereas many purebred cats have standardized coloration and markings, this emphatically does not apply to their nonpedigree counterparts. In fact, it is very unusual to see plain-colored street cats. One of their characteristics is the way in which they have variable white areas of fur on their chin and chest and often elsewhere on the body, too. The range of colors in this group tends not to be as varied, however, because of their origins. Some of today's color varieties, such as chocolate and caramel, are only likely to be encountered in pedigree cats, with the greatest variety of colors and patterns being present in the case of the Oriental breed. Even so, if you have set your heart on one of these rarer varieties, you may well need to be patient, until you can track one down.

Male or female

The other aspect that you need to consider is whether you want a male or female cat, described as a tom and queen, respectively. Toms can grow larger, and often develop the characteristic pads called jowls on their cheeks once they are mature. Queens are sometimes said to be more affectionate, but providing that your cat is neutered, there will be little evident difference between them.

Kitten or cat

Many people will almost instinctively think in terms of starting out with a young kitten, typically aged between 8 and 12 weeks. This will give an opportunity for the young cat to grow up in your home and form a close bond with you. There can also be an advantage in knowing the age of your cat with certainty, especially in terms of its veterinary care.

On the other hand, there are always more adult cats in need of homes, whose availability is also influenced by the time of year. Even cats that appear initially shy on first acquaintance can become devoted pets if you are prepared to invest time in building a bond with them, just as you would with a kitten. The only cats that will almost certainly not settle well are those that have been born wild and are described as "feral." This is why in most cases, cat-rescue organizations trap such cats and neuter them, before releasing them back into the area where they were living, rather than attempting to rehome them.

Maine Coon

Where to Find Your Cat

The choice of where to go for your new pet will have already been determined to some extent by the type of cat that you are seeking. If you want a nonpedigree kitten, you may find someone who has an unexpected litter that they want to home, either through an advertisement or a veterinary contact, although, often, it is better to make contact with a cat-rescue organization.

Purebred kittens

When it comes to obtaining a kitten from a breeder, bear in mind that the asking price generally depends not just on the breed itself, but also on the show potential of the kittens in question. Breeders have to make a judgment in this regard at an early stage, deciding which kittens in a litter they want to keep as part of their future breeding plans. The others will be offered as pets. But do not become confused by the use of the term "pet type" to describe a purebred kitten. This does not indicate that there is anything wrong with the young cat, simply that it probably has a flaw that means that it will not be suitable for exhibition purposes. Its coloration may be too dark, for example, or it may be mismarked in some way.

The risk of cats suffering from inherited illness is much lower than in the case of dogs, but there are specific tests that can be carried out today where there is a potential risk. For example, polycystic kidney disease can afflict Persians and related breeds such as Exotic Shorthairs (see page 47). Now a simple swab, taken from inside the cat's cheek, will be sufficient to provide a specimen to determine whether a particular individual is affected.

Slow growing
Some kittens in a litter, like the one in the center here, may be slightly bigger than others, but this does not necessarily mean that it will ultimately end up larger. Maine Coons grow relatively slowly, with kittens developing at different rates.

Making a decision

The Internet has made it relatively easy to find breeders, even of the more unusual cats, but do not necessarily be overly impressed by the design of a website. Other ways to track down breeders can be through cat magazines and directory advertisements. It may be worthwhile visiting shows in the area near you as well, so as to meet breeders directly, or find a club breeders' list, and contact several breeders by this means. You can then find out which, if any, have kittens available, and draw up a shortlist covering the colors on offer, gender, and price. Never be tempted to purchase a kitten without having traveled to see it first. It is quite usual to view a litter before the young cats are ready to go to a new home. If you decide to place a deposit on a particular individual, always obtain a receipt clearly stating which kitten you have chosen, and possibly photograph it at this stage as well.

Chocolate British Shorthair

Eye color changes
The eye color of kittens is blue at first and only changes gradually, being likely to end up an attractive shade in this case.

Rehoming

Do not be surprised if you are asked in some detail about your home and lifestyle before you are considered to take on a rescued kitten or cat. The key thing that the organization will want to establish in advance is that you can offer a suitable caring environment where the cat can thrive. The aim will be to match you to the right cat, so be prepared for this, too. You are far less likely to have a choice of a purebred cat in these surroundings. The overwhelming majority will be street cats. Nevertheless, even if you do not have a large budget—and some pedigree kittens, especially those of the more striking newer breeds such as the Savannah (see page 124), can be very expensive—you may be able to rehome a purebred cat.

Start by contacting breeders, as they may have some older cats that are no longer featuring in their breeding programs and are available to go to new homes. They are invariably much less expensive than kittens, largely because the demand for young cats is much greater. But you have the advantage that these older cats are already settled, and assuming they have been part of the breeder's household, they should adapt quite quickly to new surroundings.

Maine Coons

Your Kitten's Health

There is no foolproof way of being certain that the kitten or cat you choose is healthy (though certain tests can check for inherited conditions in particular breeds). But there are important steps that you can take to increase this likelihood. The most obvious if you are buying a cat is to only go to a reputable breeder who has the reputation of caring for the stock.

Early care

You should receive a diet sheet and details of the food that your kitten has been eating. Stick to this very closely for the first few weeks and only make changes gradually, once your new pet has settled in with you. This will significantly reduce the risk of digestive upsets that can potentially be fatal in a young cat. (Bear in mind that, at this age, kittens are especially vulnerable to infection.) The other information that you need are details of whether or not it has been vaccinated, with a certificate as appropriate, and when it has been dewormed. Take this information with you when you visit your chosen veterinarian for the first time with your new pet for the check up it needs soon after acquiring it.

Ears
These should be clean and free from any signs of scabs.

Nostrils
Ensure there is no discharge of any kind evident here. Kittens are prone to respiratory illnesses.

Risk of infections

Obtaining a young kitten from a shelter can be more hazardous than going to a breeder, as epidemics of respiratory disease may spread quite easily in these surroundings, with kittens especially vulnerable to the effects of cat flu in particular. Keep a close watch on the young cat at first for any signs of infection, such as runny eyes, diarrhea, loss of appetite, and the emergence of the third eyelid—this membrane can extend across the corner of each eye, when a cat loses condition. Should you suspect that your kitten could be sick, arrange an immediate veterinary check up. Its health can otherwise go into a rapid decline, with, for example, dehydration caused by diarrhea being potentially fatal to a young cat, quite apart from the infection itself.

If you obtain an older cat from a shelter and the cat's history is unknown, you need to follow a similar system. Deworming will again be essential and a course of immunizations may well be advisable to protect against killer infections such as Feline Leukemia Virus (FeLV), in the absence of any evidence that the cat has been vaccinated previously.

Mouth
Ask the breeder to open the kitten's mouth, so you can check its teeth.

Walking
The kitten should have no difficulty in walking, with its front legs held straight as it moves.

Reproductive matters

The other very important thing to consider is whether the cat has been neutered. This will be clearly apparent in the case of a tom, due to the absence of its testes, which are otherwise easily spotted below the base of the tail. In a female cat, however, the impact of such surgery will not be easily discernible in most cases, and yet it can be very important, to prevent your new cat from rapidly becoming pregnant. Cats are induced ovulators, which means that they do not have a set reproductive cycle, but release ova (eggs) in response to mating, which significantly enhances the likelihood of successful conception.

Tail
The cat should be able to move this easily, and it should not be kinked along its length.

Female cats can be neutered either through the abdominal wall on the underside of the body or via the flank. If this occurred some time ago, then the fur will have regrown, and there will be no obvious sign of the surgery. Nevertheless, a close examination may reveal the presence of scar tissue, which can create a slight ridge, confirming that the cat was neutered in the past. Seek your veterinarian's advice if you are at all uncertain.

Rear end
There should be no staining of the coat here, which would otherwise indicate a digestive disturbance.

Early days

It is equally important not to allow your cat out at first, especially with an adult individual. Young kittens are less likely to stray, but bear in mind that your new pet will not be fully protected until after it has completed its course of vaccinations, and the likelihood is that a number of cats will have passed through your yard, potentially presenting a health risk. Equally, if a kitten does stray in these surroundings, it can be hard to locate and retrieve it.

An adult cat will almost inevitably wander off if it gets out soon after arriving back home with you, ignoring your calls to return. It is absolutely vital that you keep an adult cat indoors for a period of two to three weeks, therefore, to become familiar with you before being allowed outdoors for the first time. (You will need to provide a litter tray during this period.) Always go into the yard with your pet at first and wait to feed the cat until it accompanies you back indoors again. This is a routine that you should build on so that your cat will soon start to return to you when called. The same applies in the case of kittens, once they are old enough to go outdoors.

Body profile
A pot-bellied appearance can be indicative of parasitic worms. Deworming is vital in any case.

Coat
Inspect the coat for any signs of parasites, such as fleas, which will leave dark specks in the fur.

Cat types for people who are less concerned about choosing a particular breed, but who simply want a cat that looks stunning.

(Left to right) Blue, Cream Tabby, Brown Tabby, Tortoiseshell

Colorful Cats

Cats have been created in a very wide range of colors, far removed from the rather grayish, striped appearance of their wild ancestor, the European Wild Cat (*Felis silvestris silvestris*). The tabby markings are gone, creating what are sometimes described as "self-colored" (solid-colored) cats. There is a clear divide in the way that the colors cropped up within the domestic cat population, however, and it has been possible for researchers to map their origins to some extent. This has entailed looking at the proportions of individual colors in populations of nonpedigree cats in different areas.

As a result, it has emerged that there were two centers of origin for cats displaying red coloration. The first was discovered in Turkey, and from there, such cats probably radiated out to parts of eastern Europe and into Asia as well. A second area of the world where cats of this color tended to predominate in the local cat population was discovered in Scandinavia. A third was in the northern isles of Scotland, but the researchers thought that it was more likely that such cats were introduced to these islands by Viking seafarers, rather than actually originating there.

Selective breeding of cats in different parts of the world has also given vital clues as to where today's colors originally occurred. It is clear that chocolate and lilac coloration arose in Southeast Asia, centuries before cats displaying these colors were seen in the West.

1. White

There are distinct types of white cats, although the differences between them can be concealed in their genes rather than being immediately evident. Nevertheless, eye coloration is significant, as blue-eyed and odd-eyed white cats are sometimes deaf.

History

White is now a color commonly associated with various breeds, although it is decidedly rare in nonpedigrees. In some cases, such as the white American Shorthair shown here, the eyes may be of different colors, indicating a so-called "odd-eyed white." There are also blue-eyed whites, and white cats with eyes that may vary in color from green to orange. In the case of young kittens, however, bear in mind that their eyes will naturally be blue at this early stage, and their true coloration will only become apparent by the time they are approaching one month old.

Health issues

White cats are at risk from sunburn and skin cancer, because they lack any protective melanin pigment in their skin. The tips of their ears are especially vulnerable, with crusty inflammation here being a warning sign. Using sunblock for cats is not generally recommended, because they can wipe this off with their front legs when grooming and may swallow it, and products sold for human usage can be toxic to them. However, there are safe sunblocks available for cats.

Deafness
Hearing in the case of odd-eyed whites will be normal on the side of the head opposite the blue eye.

Underfoot
Even the paws are pink, reflecting the absence of melanin, which is responsible for dark coloration.

Appearance of fur
The fur is pure white in color and does not have a yellowish hue associated with it.

Tail
Since the tail is well furred, this helps provide protection from the Sun's rays. Sunburn affects exposed areas of skin.

2. Cream

Cream is the lightest color variety seen in domestic cats, but the depth of coloration is variable, even between littermates. Experienced breeders may not always be able to predict with accuracy which kittens will have the palest coats as adults.

AT A GLANCE
- Cream coloration varies in depth
- Tabby patterning may be evident
- Attractive coppery-orange eyes
- Longhaired and shorthaired varieties

Head pattern
A consistent tabby marking is the faint M-shaped patterning on the head.

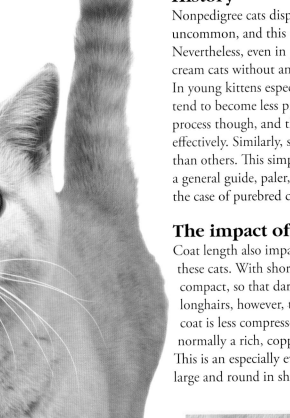

History

Nonpedigree cats displaying areas of cream coloration are not uncommon, and this color is now present in many breeds today. Nevertheless, even in pedigree lineages, it is very difficult to breed cream cats without any traces of tabby markings on their bodies. In young kittens especially, these darker lines show up clearly but tend to become less prominent as the cat matures. This is a random process though, and there is nothing that can be done to control it effectively. Similarly, some cream cats are described as being "hotter" than others. This simply refers to their more reddish coloration. As a general guide, paler, even coloration is to be preferred, certainly in the case of purebred cats.

The impact of coat length

Coat length also impacts on the presence of markings in these cats. With shorthaired individuals, the coat is quite compact, so that dark and light banding shows up clearly. In longhairs, however, the contrast tends not to be as clear, as the coat is less compressed. Eye color in the case of cream cats is normally a rich, coppery-orange shade that enhances their appeal. This is an especially evident feature, with the eyes of these cats large and round in shape.

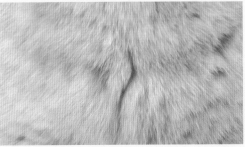

Barring
Tabby markings are highly variable on the legs.

Plain toes
Markings become less evident toward the toes.

3. Red

Red cats are highly sought after, because of their striking appearance. Just like creams they usually show tabby markings, especially as kittens, although these markings will generally fade with age. There are both longhaired and shorthaired breeds that display this coloration.

AT A GLANCE

- Stunning rich red coloration
- Nonpedigree cats usually paler
- Red recognized in many breeds
- Majority are males

Shades of red

There is a distinctive difference today between the appearance of purebred and nonpedigree examples in this case. This is a reflection of the distinctive variation that exists in the depth of red coloration between them. When such cats were first recognized for exhibition purposes, back in the late 1800s, they were described as orange. Since then, however, selective breeding has now resulted in pedigree cats, such as this example here, that have a much deeper, redder coat than their ordinary pet counterparts, explaining the change in name. In contrast, nonpedigree cats with similar, paler coloration are typically described as ginger. It is quite usual also for them to display more prominent tabby markings, too. The area under the chin is often white as well.

Gender considerations

There is a close relationship between red and tortoiseshell cats, with red being a sex-linked color as far as genetic inheritance is concerned. While red males can be produced from a pairing involving either a male or female cat carrying the red gene, both parents must do so in the hope of producing a red female. This is why the majority of red cats are male, with females of this color much rarer. Even so, they are more common than male tortoiseshells, and they are fertile. Therefore, always check a red kitten carefully, to be sure of its gender.

Ruff color
The ruff of longer fur may be paler in color.

Dark spots
The fur at the base of each whisker is an especially dark shade of red.

Patterning
Tabby markings are far less apparent in longhairs than in shorthairs.

4. Lilac

Unlike the situation with most colors, where nonpedigree cats helped shape the early pedigree bloodlines, this has not occurred in the case of lilac varieties. Crossbreeding between Western and Eastern breeds has been necessary to transfer this trait.

AT A GLANCE

- Frosty gray shade
- Pinkish hue to the coat
- Relatively new color from Asia
- Now seen in a number of breeds

History

Lilac is a relatively recent addition to the colors associated with cat breeds in the West, especially in the case of self-colored (solid) individuals. Nevertheless, such cats have been recorded in Asia for centuries, as typified by the lilac form of the Korat, known today as the Thai Lilac. (These cats are not called lilac Korats, though, simply because the description of Korat means "blue cat.") The absence of lilac as a color in nonpedigree cats elsewhere means that examples of ordinary individuals displaying lilac coloration are rarely seen. The situation is also unlikely to change, as this would require a number of random matings with pedigree cats. Therefore, if you want a lilac cat, then you need to look at purebred options.

Distinctions

It is not always that easy to distinguish between lilac and blue cats, especially when they are kittens. Look closely at the nose, as this should be pinkish in a lilac cat, as well as the paw pads. The coat is a light shade of frosty gray with a pinkish hue, which is especially apparent in bright light. Lilac represents the dilute form of chocolate coloration in cats, just as cream is the dilute counterpart of red.

Appearance
Lilac is a warmer shade than blue, due to its pinkish hue.

Facial features
Prominent jowls below the jaw indicate a mature male cat.

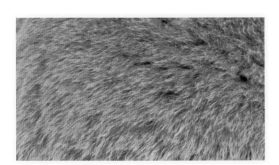

Coat
Coat type should resemble that of the particular breed concerned.

5. Chocolate

Rich, dark chocolate brown coloration is highly prized in the cat world, and it has now been introduced successfully to a number of breeds, ranging from British Shorthairs to Persian Longhairs, by crossbreeding with cats of Asian origins.

AT A GLANCE

- Distinctive brown coloration
- Variable eye color
- Seen in both longhaired and shorthaired
- A color of Asian origin

History

Being the result of relatively recent breeding programs in Europe, North America, and elsewhere, chocolate cats do not correspond as closely to type as other more established varieties. Most significantly, they tend to be somewhat smaller in size, which may be a reflection of their Asian origins. Breeders are now concentrating on improving the breed characteristics, having transfered this color into their existing bloodlines. This may make it easier to track down a chocolate individual that will make an ideal pet, even if it is lacking in show qualities. Chocolate nonpedigree cats are highly unusual, simply because outside Asia, this is not a "natural" color within the domestic cat population.

Recognition

Young chocolate kittens are a light, milk chocolate color at birth, and they darken as they grow older. The nose coloration is brownish with a pinkish hue in a good light, as are the paw pads. The eyes are generally greenish, but the depth of this coloration can vary, and in some cases, it can be yellowish instead. In the case of longhaired cats, the ruff of longer fur under the neck will be paler than that elsewhere on the body. The appearance of shorthaired chocolate cats is more consistent. They generally display a much more even depth of coloration.

Short coat
The coat tends to be darker where the fur is shorter on the face and legs.

Consistency
There should be no trace of tabby markings on the tail or elsewhere.

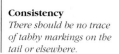

Uneven color
Chocolate coloration may not be even in the case of longhaired cats.

6. Blue

Blue fur in cats is effectively gray, rather than being a more typical shade of blue. This is because it represents the diluted form of black, in terms of feline coloration. As such, the depth of blue can vary markedly.

AT A GLANCE

- A very popular color
- Grayish rather than blue
- Depth of color can vary
- Eye color green or orange

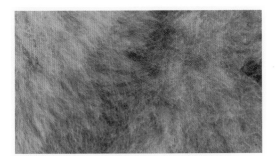

History

Blue is a well-established color, as it is associated with many breeds and actually defines some, notably the Chartreux (see page 107) and the Korat (see page 97). Coat type does, however, influence its appearance, and there can be a silvery sheen associated with it, especially in good light. This is most apparent in shorthaired blue cats, especially those without a dense, bulky undercoat such as the blue form of the Russian breed, formerly known as the Russian Blue. This effect is created by the presence of lighter silvery tips to the guard hairs, which create a glistening effect when the cat moves.

Breeding

The genetics of dilute colors such as blue mean that the only way to be certain of obtaining kittens of this color is to pair together two blues. This is because blue is an autosomal recessive character, and mating a blue with a cat of another color will only result in blues in their litter if the other cat is carrying the blue gene. This will not be discernible visually. In some cases, notably Persian Longhairs, the depth of blue coloration can be quite varied among individuals. This can be evident even in the case of littermates. As a general rule, cats displaying lighter blue coloration are preferred.

Nose
Blue nose, with the paw pads corresponding in color.

Coloration
This needs to be even over the body.

Tail
This should be free from tabby markings in adult cats.

7. Black

These cats have more folklore attached to them than cats of any other color, and they have often been linked with witchcraft. In reality, a black cat, in the guise of a Persian Longhair, was the first variety ever to be given a show standard.

History

Cats of this color should be a rich, jet-black, as shown by this Oriental, whose appearance is enhanced by its short, sleek coat. In contrast, black Persian Longhairs tend not to display such striking black coloration, simply because their coats are not as compact, and they also have a thick undercoat. Nevertheless, the intense black coloration can change, depending on the weather. Black cats that are allowed outdoors often develop a slightly rusty hue, particularly on their backs and sides. This is caused by the bleaching effect of bright sunlight. It will not be a permanent feature, with the coat's appearance restored to normal after the next molt.

Pedigree vs. nonpedigree

One of the features that sets pedigree cats apart is their coloration. In the case of black purebred cats, irrespective of the breed, there will be no areas of white in the fur. This is virtually never the case in nonpedigree cats, where sporadic white hairs are randomly distributed throughout the coat, and there are frequently larger white areas here, too. In contrast to the situation with dogs, cats will not develop gray hairs as they grow older, and so do not show their age.

Head shape
Orientals have a triangular-shaped head, reflecting their Siamese ancestry.

Paw color
The paw pads, as well as the nose, are jet-black.

Balance
The depth of black coloration is consistent over the entire coat.

8. Oriental Caramel

This is an unusual color, that originated in the Oriental breed, and the gene has since been transferred to British Shorthair bloodlines, although caramel individuals in general are still scarce at present. In the early days, such cats were described as pastels.

AT A GLANCE

- Rare color
- Complex breeding
- Different appearance between Orientals and Burmese
- New addition to British Shorthair bloodlines

History

Breeding of caramel cats is relatively complex, given the nature of the gene responsible for this coloration. It effectively acts to transform what would otherwise be a cat of another color—fawn, lilac, or blue—into a caramel. They do not have to be simply self-colored (solid), either, as the gene will also combine with tabby patterning and can also exert its influence in the case of tortoiseshell cats. It has to be said that caramel cats have not caused great excitement, especially in the Oriental category, where there are many different color variants and combinations. Such cats have a bluish-fawn appearance, and as they mature, the sleek coat may also acquire a metallic sheen. Their coloration is consistent over the body, not becoming paler on the underparts as in the Burmese (see page 56).

Burmese breeding

The variety has not established a strong following in other breeds, either, with the caramel form of the Burmese still being essentially confined to New Zealand where it was created by the ongoing efforts of a geneticist in a breeding program that began during the mid-1970s. It is now clear, though, that the actual coloration of these cats depends on their parentage, with their underlying background color, such as lilac, being significant. In caramel Burmese, too, their underparts are paler. They tend to be pale fawn, with honey-yellow underparts, and an evident lilac suffusion.

Ears
Pale skin inside the large ears that usually characterize Orientals.

Appearance
Slight traces of tabby barring are apparent on this individual.

Tail
The relatively long, tapering tail displays even coloration along its length.

9. Dilute Calico

Also known as the blue-cream tortoiseshell and white, cats displaying this type of coloration are virtually always female, for genetic reasons. Any males that do occur are the result of a rare chromosomal abnormality, and they will prove to be sterile.

AT A GLANCE
- Highly individual patterning
- Can be purebred
- Almost inevitably female
- Friendly nature

History

One of the most distinctive features of these cats is their highly individual patterning, which means that even among littermates and pedigree bloodlines, there will not be two kittens showing matching markings. The colors in this case are cream and blue, which explains why they are sometimes known as dilute tortoiseshell and white, simply because these colors are the paler counterparts of red and black coloration, respectively, which are the tortoiseshell's traditional colors. These cats, like other tortoiseshells, have a reputation for being friendly by nature and also making good mothers. Longhaired tortoiseshells will look most spectacular in the winter, when the coat is at its most profuse, with a ruff of longer fur around the neck.

Showing

The random nature of the markings also means that they are usually completely asymmetric, and even for breeders of show cats, it is impossible to predict the markings. At one extreme, a kitten may be almost entirely white, while at the other, it may have just a small, white patch of fur. This means that breeding them for exhibition purposes requires more luck than usual, in order to ensure that they meet the required show standard for the breed concerned. This cannot be predicted with any certainty from the mother's appearance.

Staying the same
The patterning of this young cat will not alter as it grows older.

Paler below
White areas tend to occur on the chest, with colored fur on the sides of the body.

Recognizable markings
Markings are not consistent in tortoiseshell cats of any variety.

10. Tortoiseshell

Tortoiseshells are among the most colorful of all cats, with their coats consisting of blotches and swirls of contrasting red and black fur, offset against bright orange eyes. This patterning occurs in both shorthaired and longhaired breeds, as well as nonpedigrees.

History

As in the case of other tortoiseshell varieties, the appearance of such cats is highly individual. This means that it is possible to enjoy the company of a particular pedigree cat and yet have a truly individual companion at the same time. None of these cats are exactly alike. Standardization in this case is based on the type of cat—its distinctive features as a recognizable breed—rather than on its individual coloration. Kittens will not change in this regard as they grow older, although they may lose any hints of tabby patterning present in the reddish areas of the coat.

Why female?

Tortoiseshells are normally female, being born in litters alongside red- and black-colored male kittens. The incidence of male tortoiseshell cats has been estimated at 1 in 3,000 births, because of the way that this characteristic is inherited. It is linked to the sex chromosomes, which also determine the cat's gender. Males normally have only one X chromosome alongside a shorter Y one, whereas females have paired X sex chromosomes. Male tortoiseshells result when there is an extra X chromosome, however, causing them to have an XXY configuration, which also renders them sterile.

Eyes
Eye coloration depends on the individual, and ranges from yellow through orange to green.

Hidden beneath
The underlying skin also reflects the difference in coat coloration.

Mixing up coloration
Brindling is the name given to areas where the colors mix.

Cat types for people who are seeking individuality in their pets, with the markings of cats in this group being particularly distinctive.

Dilute Tortoiseshell and White

Patterned Cats

Most cats today possess patterning of some type on their coats, in common with their wild relatives. Tabby patterning serves a purpose in nature, helping break up the cat's outline in a wooded environment and allowing it to merge more effectively into the background. Zoologists describe this as "disruptive camouflage," although to our eyes, the patterning associated with domestic cats is not functional but simply esthetically appealing. Nevertheless, it does make it easier in some cases for cats to hunt successfully, as they are less conspicuous to their potential prey.

Patterning can appear in all varieties, with the sole exception of pure-white individuals. Aside from the range of tabby markings, there are also patched colors. It is quite feasible for there to be more than one type of patterning on an individual as well, as in the case of calico torbies, where tortoiseshell-and-white patterning is combined with tabby markings. Not all patterns are permanent in cats—notably as far as colorpoint varieties such as the Siamese are concerned. These can be affected both by temperature and the cat's age. Patterning does not just affect parts of the body, either. It can also extend down individual hairs, having a marked impact on an individual's appearance, as in the case of ticked tabbies.

Silver Tabby

1. Lilac Bicolored Ragdoll

More myths surround this breed than any other. The Ragdoll was originally developed in the U.S. during the 1960s, but it has since built up an international following and has become a very popular choice as a family pet.

History

The breed's creator, Ann Baker, suggested that these cats were immune to pain. This generated considerable publicity but was untrue. They became known as Ragdolls because of the way they relaxed when being picked up, just like a doll of this type. By combining what were effectively two of the most placid breeds in the cat world—in the guise of the Persian Longhair and Birman (see page 45)—it is not surprising that the Ragdoll has such an appealing nature. Neither of these ancestral breeds possesses strong hunting instincts, either, with the result being that Ragdolls are likely to leave local wildlife unmolested. This trait has led them to become popular in Australia. Ragdolls were first seen in Europe in 1981, when four were imported to the U.K.

Color variants

The traditional colors associated with this breed are seal, blue, lilac, and chocolate, although more recently, red and cream have been added to this list. They can be acquired with self-colored (solid) points, as well as lynx (tabby) and tortie points, plus torbies points, which are a combination of tortie and lynx points on the same cat. Although the coat is not prone to matting, Ragdolls should still be groomed at least twice a week. The coat is relatively short in young Ragdolls but it is still a good idea to start grooming them at this stage so they get used to the experience. It also helps build a bond between you.

Size
These are very large cats, with males bigger than females.

Coat
Not especially long, nor especially inclined to mat.

Chilled out
Ragdolls have a very relaxed nature, making them ideal pets.

2. Classic Tabby

Although described as the classic tabby pattern, suggesting that it was the original tabby form of the domestic cat, this is actually a form that was not described until the 1600s. It is thought to have arisen as a mutation.

History

This type of tabby patterning has been refined in purebred cats such as the American Shorthair, so it stands out very clearly. It is also described as blotched tabby, because the markings consist largely of darker blotches on a lighter background color. The most prominent blotches are present on the flanks at the top of each hind leg, and each should resemble an oyster in shape. More random patterning is characteristic of nonpedigree tabbies of this type. There is a typical M-shaped marking on the forehead, with stripes encircling the legs and running down the back. The tail consists of alternating light and dark rings and ends in a dark tip. The same applies in other tabbies, too.

Colors

This individual is a brown tabby, with its markings being black. High contrast is also a feature of silver tabbies, where this pattern is superimposed on a silvery body color. Red classic tabbies are different, however, because they have dark red markings set against a lighter red body color, but the contrast is still clearly evident. In other cases, such as cream or blue, the patterning is not as distinctive.

Upfront
Markings on the shoulders are often referred to as butterfly patterning because of their shape.

Pedigree distinction
In purebred classic tabbies, the black areas do not have any brown hairs present and the markings on the tail tend to be more even.

Chin
A white chin is a typical feature associated with this variety.

3. Mackerel Tabby

The mackerel is the original form of the tabby, displaying a characteristic striped pattern. This was said to resemble the skeleton of the mackerel, which is why this fish's name was appended to the description of cats of this type.

AT A GLANCE
- Common in both pedigree and nonpedigree cats
- Associated with many colors
- Hardy cats
- Patterning shows better in shorthairs

History

Mackerel tabby patterning is the most common tabby variant in cats. It can be seen in both shorthaired and longhaired cats, but its impact is again the most striking in cats with short fur, as in this case. This causes the markings to stand out strongly. Patterning of this type is very common in ordinary nonpedigree cats, and in some cases, it can be broken up by white areas on the body. Even in the case of purebred individuals, breeding individuals with ideal markings is not easy and can prove to be a lottery. The lines running down each side of the body should be evenly spaced.

Breeding tabbies

The gene responsible for mackerel tabby patterning is the same one as seen in the European Wild Cat (*Felis silvestris silvestris*), being inherited from the domestic cat's ancestor. In contrast, blotched tabby patterning results from a recessive mutation. This means that if a mackerel tabby and a blotched tabby mate, then their kittens will all be mackerel tabbies. Only if two kittens carrying the blotched tabby gene mate will this trait re-emerge in their offspring. Tabbies are generally friendly cats, but they are less common in exhibition circles, because of the difficulties in breeding well-marked individuals. Nevertheless, there are few cats more striking in appearance, especially when there is good contrast in the coat. Their markings will not change with maturity.

Tail pattern
This consists of a series of light and dark rings, especially evident on the sides.

Appearance
Lines on the body may not be continuous, often broken toward the underparts.

Variations
Tabby patterning on the legs is not symmetrical or consistent.

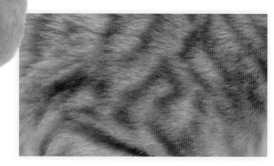

4. Spotted Tabby

It is said that the first spotted tabbies were bred in ancient Egypt, and this patterning is also not uncommon in wild cats. Spotted domestic cats are largely purebred, however, with such markings less common in nonpedigrees.

AT A GLANCE

- Impressive appearance
- Individual patterning
- Clarity of markings significant
- Purebred spotted tabbies more common

History

Spotted tabby patterning is believed to have resulted from the mackerel tabby, due to a genetic effect that has broken up the characteristic stripes into a series of spots, especially over the body. These can vary in size and are often not strictly circular but may have a slightly elongated appearance. Tabby markings elsewhere on the body, such as the head, legs, and tail, are essentially unaffected, remaining as a series of stripes or rings, with the tip of the tail dark. Just as with other tabby forms, this pattern is most apparent in the case of shorthaired breeds, especially in cases such as the Oriental, which lacks a dense undercoat.

Individuals

The silver spotted tabby, as shown here, is especially popular, thanks to the contrast between the silvery ground color and the black tabby patterning, but a wide range of other varieties exist. In most cases, however, the cat's markings are simply a darker reflection of the underlying ground color. The subtlety of the spotted patterning may become less distinctive when the cat is shedding its coat, but the actual patterning will be a consistent feature throughout its life.

Spotted overview
The spots must be clearly defined and ideally should not overlap.

Tail
An even pattern of rings along its length is preferred.

Legs
Barring extends down the legs but should not extend to the toes.

5. Oriental Ticked Tabby

Ticked tabbies are distinct from the three preceding tabby varieties. Tabby patterning does not indicate a specific type of cat, though, but simply describes particular markings that can be seen in various breeds, such as the Oriental (as shown).

AT A GLANCE
- Distinctive appearance
- Ticking is associated with many colors
- Markings highly individual
- Barring may be entirely absent

History

The effect of the ticked tabby mutation is quite unmistakable. Gone are the bars and stripes, with very little trace of them remaining, aside from on the extremities of the body. Instead, the individuals will display alternating light and dark bands on their hair, which is responsible for the so-called "ticking," which is most evident when the cat moves. Ticked tabby patterning is also to be seen in nonpedigree cats—especially in Southeast Asia, which is where the Singapura breed (see page 88) originated. Although again most pronounced in shorthaired cats, ticked tabby longhairs also exist—most notably in the case of the Somali (see page 101).

A different type

Studies have shown that the ticked tabby is a completely separate mutation and unrelated to other tabby patterns. Nevertheless, if present, it blocks these other tabby patterns from being expressed visually. Each hair should have two or three bands of ticking along its length, with the darkest area of the coat along the back. The color of the pattern on the tail, legs, and head should correspond to that of the ticking. As in other cases, the pattern of barring on the legs is highly individual, enabling a cat to be easily recognized. The ringed pattern on the tail is variable, too.

Tail
The solid dark line running down the back can extend along the tail.

Underparts
The sides and underside of the body are paler than the back. This cat also has a skull-cap rather than a clear M-shaped marking on the head.

Legs
Barring may be present here, but it is not a consistent feature in ticked tabbies.

6. Calico

The patterning in the case of the calico, also called the tortoiseshell and white, is entirely random, although as in this particular case, there may be a so-called white "blaze" present, extending between the eyes down to the nose.

AT A GLANCE

- Unique appearance
- Both purebred and nonpedigree choices
- Likely to be female
- Not generally aggressive

History

The most significant difference between nonpedigree and purebred calico individuals is that the colors will be more clearly defined in the latter group, with no odd white hairs cropping up in black areas of the coat, for example. The colors in the calico are shades of red and cream, offset against black-and-white areas that are equally variable in extent. As in the case of other tortoiseshell varieties, males are virtually unknown in this instance and are sterile on the rare occasions when they do crop up. Such individuals are otherwise quite healthy and normal and will make good pets. Calicos have a reputation for being long-lived. There are a number of other calico varieties as well, deriving from different forms of tortoiseshell. They include the dilute calico, which features blue-cream and white patterning.

Patterning

The appearance of these cats is highly individual, which can be useful if you live in an area where there are a number of cats. You can then very easily spot your pet from a distance—this may be less straightforward with an ordinary tabby. Calico patterning tends not to be as intense in the case of a longhaired cat, compared with a shorthaired individual, due to the lie of the fur. The result is that since the coat is not as compact, the individual hairs do not lie in such close proximity to each other. This is what causes the coloration to be less intense.

Ears
Black on the edge of the ear means the ear tuft is black, too.

Variations
Nose color can vary, depending on the color of the surrounding coat.

Down below
White coloration tends to predominate on the chest.

7. Torbie and White

The description of torbie and white is a shorthand way of referring to a tortoiseshell tabby-and-white cat. This individual is therefore almost certainly a female, thanks to its tortoiseshell appearance, on top of which tabby markings are superimposed.

AT A GLANCE
- Unique patterning
- Generally a female cat
- Friendly, affectionate nature
- Easily recognized

History

Torbie and white is not a particular breed but simply a pattern that can be encountered in a number of cats ranging from American Shorthairs (see page 104) through to Persian Longhairs. The distribution of the tortoiseshell-and-white patterning is random, and this in turn affects the tabby markings, too, because these will not be evident in white areas of the coat. Nevertheless, in common with other forms of tabby, there will almost certainly be tabby markings on the forehead, as well as on the legs and tail. The appearance of torbie and whites is unique and unpredictable too, as far as kittens are concerned, although their markings will not change significantly after birth.

The potential

All tortoiseshell-and-white variants can occur as torbies. The use of Orientals (see page 63) has opened up exciting possibilities, permitting the breeding of cinnamon tortoiseshell-and-white tabbies among others. Furthermore, these cats can display either classic or mackerel tabby patterning, with prominent blotches on the sides of the body, as distinct from discrete lines, indicating the classic variant. Ideally, there will be relatively little white fur, so as not to obscure the tabby markings.

Nose
The color is varied, showing traces of black as well as red.

Tail mix
Calico (tortoiseshell-and-white) coloration is very evident here.

Leg barring
Darker red tabby markings are clearly visible.

8. Siamese

The Siamese is the best-known example of the so-called colorpointed breeds. The term "points" refers to the body extremities, comprising the face, ears, legs, feet, and tail, with these areas of the body generally being of a darker color than the remainder of the body.

History

The Siamese's name gives a clue to its origins, as it was first recorded in the Southeast Asian country of Thailand, which used to be known as Siam. Newborn Siamese kittens are white, but within a few days, they start to display the distinctive coloration on their points, which will then intensify. This characteristic is temperature-dependent, with these extremities being slightly cooler than the cat's core body temperature. Bandaging a limb can, however, affect the patterning, causing the coat here to become paler than the other points, as the temperature is raised. In older Siamese cats, as their circulation becomes less effective, so too the body color itself will start to darken, spoiling their show potential. This will be apparent over the flanks, being indicative of a slight decrease in body temperature.

Personality

Siamese cats are very athletic, lively cats and will benefit from being given a climbing frame indoors, because otherwise there is a risk that they might try to climb up the curtains and cause damage. Be prepared to keep valuable items in cabinets, too! Highly affectionate and demonstrative, Siamese are real extroverts. Four traditional colors are recognized. These are blue point, lilac point, seal point, and chocolate point, but over recent years, others, including red points, have been created.

Profile
Siamese are relatively small cats with an athletic build.

Eyes
The eyes of adult Siamese are always this attractive shade of blue.

Nose
The color of the nose corresponds to that of the points.

9. Chinchilla Persian

The distinctive appearance of the Chinchilla Persian stems from the dark patterning present at the tips of the long guard hairs in its coat. This contrasts not just with the pale areas on the rest of the guard hairs themselves, but also with the unpigmented undercoat.

AT A GLANCE

- Sparkling appearance
- Relaxed, friendly nature
- Attractive eyes
- Require regular daily grooming

History

The Chinchilla Persian is named after the South American rodent that has highly prized fur with a similar, albeit darker, appearance. In the case of the cat, the subtle sparkling evident on the coat results from black tipping. This extends just a short distance down each hair from the tip, covering the upperparts of the body, including the head, back, and tail, as well as the flanks. In contrast, the area of the underparts from the chin down on to the chest and along the abdomen is pure white, without any tipping, and this applies to the area of the hind legs below the hocks. There must be no trace of any tabby markings or cream coloration.

Stunning eyes

The Chinchilla Persian's appeal is reinforced by its eyes, which can range from emerald to blue-green. Black pigmentation on the eyelids serves to highlight them, acting rather like eye liner. The nose is a contrasting pinkish shade, again outlined with a black border. In terms of overall size, Chinchilla Persians tend to be smaller than many other varieties within the Persian group. They need regular daily grooming, not just to stop their coat from becoming matted, but also to minimize the amount of hair shed around the home.

On the move
The shimmering effect is most evident when the cat is walking.

Ears
As in the case of other Persians, the ears are relatively small.

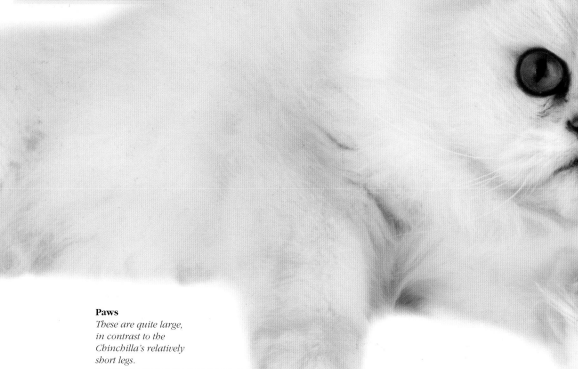

Paws
These are quite large, in contrast to the Chinchilla's relatively short legs.

10. Shaded Silver

Although it may not seem immediately obvious, the shaded silver is similar in some respects to the Chinchilla Persian seen opposite. It, too, is a "tipped" variety, but, in this case, the tipping is more extensive, extending farther down the individual hairs.

AT A GLANCE

- Attractive coloration
- Longhaired and shorthaired options
- Distinctive appearance
- Tabby ancestry

Nose and eyes
The nose is pinkish in color, with dark rims around the eyes.

Undercoat
The white undercoat serves to emphasize the contrast with the tipping.

History

These cats were originally bred from poorly marked silver tabby stock, which was crossed with smokes. In the early days, both Chinchillas and shaded silvers were characterized by orange eyes, with the green eyes seen in such cats today regarded as a fault. The long coat on the body of this cat ensures that it is not possible for the tabby patterning to break through, although longhaired shaded silvers may be born with tabby markings evident here, having shorter coats at this stage. Tabby markings are often to be seen through where the coat is short, as on the legs.

Other variants

The silver forms—in terms of shaded and Chinchilla—are most commonly seen, but there are other color variants of this type, too. Their blue counterparts (a dilute form of silver) actually look very similar, and these two colors can be difficult to separate in adult cats, once the pigmentation has become more diffuse. Chocolate forms have also been bred. Paler versions, including cats with cream tipping, have also been recorded. The cream form is more impressive in a shaded form, because there is more contrasting coloring evident in the coat.

Tail
The tipping is evident in the tail as well as on the body, with no tabby rings here.

Birman

Cat types for people who like to have a very affectionate pet that will spend plenty of time with them.

Lap Cats

All cats are affectionate, but there are some breeds that tend to be more people-focused than others. The creation of cats specially bred for temperament and friendliness is a relatively recent development, however. It is not just about breeding, though—neutering is important, too. This should ensure that your cat is less likely to stray, especially in the case of males who can otherwise end up wandering over a considerable distance through the neighborhood and who are also more likely to be injured in fights. The age for neutering depends to some extent on the breed, as some such as the Siamese (see page 86) mature earlier, with females of these breeds occasionally being able to mate successfully at just four months old. However, six to nine months is the average age of maturity for most cats.

As your cat becomes older, do not be surprised if it proves to be less inclined to sleep on your lap. You may notice that it becomes reluctant to settle down here, especially for any length of time, preferring instead to sleep alongside you. This is a reflection of the fact that its joints are probably not as flexible as they used to be, and so resting in this way is no longer comfortable. What you could try is to obtain a soft cushion for your cat, and place this over your lap, as it should provide more support.

Burmilla

1. Abyssinian

Intelligent, affectionate, and adaptable, Abyssinians make excellent companions. They have an attractive, elegant appearance, with their short coats meaning that their grooming needs are minimal. These cats will settle well in a family environment, not being fazed by either children or dogs.

History

The breed is named after the African country of Abyssinia—now known as Ethiopia. The first example seen in Europe, called Zula, was reputedly brought back by a soldier serving as part of the British Army. It is thought that the actual origins of the breed may lie to the north, however, in Egypt. Its subsequent development then took place in England initially, with such cats represented at one of the earliest cat shows, held in 1871 at Crystal Palace near London. At this stage, the cats still retained tabby barring on their legs, which has since been eliminated by selective breeding. Prominent ears tufts were probably more commonly seen in those early days, emphasizing their exotic appearance.

Breed development

The traditional color of the breed is still called "the usual" in the U.K., being referred to as "the ruddy" in the U.S. It is a rich golden-brown color, with a ruddy undercoat and distinct black ticking. A range of new colors have now been created. These include blue, fawn, chocolate, and lilac, as well as equivalent silver variants such as the blue-silver. Abyssinians suffered badly as a result of Feline Leukemia Virus (FeLV) infections, but now thankfully, there is a vaccine available, and in common with all cats, members of this breed should be protected against this potentially fatal illness, for which there is no treatment.

Chin
White fur is commonly seen here, but this is not encouraged as far as exhibition stock is concerned.

AT A GLANCE
- Affectionate, friendly nature
- Thrives on human company
- A ticked tabby variant
- Bred in an increasing range of colors

Ticked tabby
The patterning is essentially confined to the individual hairs, rather than resulting in solid tabby markings.

Legs and feet
These are quite slender and delicate, compared with the body profile.

FELINE CHARACTERISTICS		NOTES
Starting out	Bred in an increasing range of color varieties. Kittens quite easily obtainable.	Generally small litter sizes.
Personality	Playful cats, yet not especially noisy by nature.	
Appearance	Quite an exotic appearance, especially in cats that have ear tufts.	
At home	Settles well, proving home-loving and affectionate.	
Behavior	Makes a good family pet, either for people on their own or as part of a family.	Generally gets along well with dogs, but not to be trusted with small pets or birds.
Grooming	Smooth coat, needs very little grooming to remain immaculate.	
Common health issues	Susceptible to Feline Leukemia (FeLV), seemingly having little resistance.	Vaccination essential to guard against this killer infection.

2. Birman

The Birman is something of a cat of mystery, as far as its origins are concerned, but it is a devoted companion, thriving in domestic surroundings. Since it lacks a dense undercoat, grooming of this longhaired breed is not difficult.

AT A GLANCE

- Stunning blue-eyed companion
- Gentle and home-loving
- Loyal by nature
- Well-defined markings

FELINE CHARACTERISTICS		NOTES
Starting out	A rare breed of Asian origins, shaped almost entirely in the West.	It can take over two years for the full color of these cats to become apparent.
Personality	Friendly, relaxed nature, forming a close bond with its family members.	
Appearance	A pointed, semi-longhaired breed with white areas on the front and hind feet.	Very difficult to breed with the ideal patterning present.
At home	Not a noisy breed, in spite of its Oriental origins, and an easy-going companion.	
Behavior	Not especially interested in hunting, but enjoys playing and chasing toys.	Generally gets along well with dogs.
Grooming	Needs to be carried out several times a week, especially when shedding.	
Common health issues	Renal problems can be an issue, with Birmans sometimes having smaller kidneys than normal.	

History

In their Burmese homeland, the Birman's ancestors were kept in temples, where they were regarded as the reincarnations of deceased monks. Two Europeans were given a pair of these cats, for helping repel an attack on the Temple of Lao-Tsun during the mid-1920s. Only the female reached France alive, and she gave birth to kittens. All subsequent Birmans are said to trace their ancestry back to these two individuals, although almost certainly, outcrosses to other breeds helped broaden the bloodline. Recently, cat enthusiasts who have gained access to Tibet have described seeing cats there with similar markings.

Tail
Point coloration begins to develop once the kittens are about two weeks old.

Eyes
Rounded in shape and always rich blue in color.

Pattern and color

The white areas on the Birman's front paws are known as gloves, with this patterning more extensive on the hind legs, extending up to the level of the hocks. These hind limb markings are referred to as boots and must also be symmetrical. For many years, only seal-point Birmans were recognized, and then the blue point was created, as a result of crossings with Persian Longhairs that introduced this color. A wide selection of other varieties have since been created, although not all are yet recognized for show purposes.

Feet
The darkest area of color is just above the gloves.

3. British Shorthair

British Shorthairs have built up a worldwide following, thanks to their friendly, easygoing temperament. Their stunning good looks have resulted in these cats being used in various advertising campaigns, too. They are affectionate by nature, as well as being relatively quiet and placid.

History

In the second half of the 1800s, when cat showing was just starting, breeders concentrated on refining ordinary street cats, to create varieties for this purpose. They set out to breed cats that are self-colored (solid), displaying no white areas in their coat, and also aimed to increase their size. This latter characteristic was achieved by matings involving Persian Longhairs. New colors have also been created by crossbreeding, with chocolate and cinnamon being some of the newest British Shorthair varieties to be created. Colorpointed British Shorthairs have also been bred over recent years, with their pointed appearance introduced via Himalayan stock. Even though they now look significantly different, British Shorthairs still retain a temperament like that of an ordinary nonpedigree cat.

Their appeal

The adaptability of the British Shorthair is such that it can be kept as an apartment cat, and it has a playful nature. Members of the breed learn quickly, explaining in part why they are popular with animal trainers for commercials and movies. British Shorthairs have what is best described as a cheery disposition, and they may follow you around, to see what you are doing. They are keen observers. Their calm nature means that they will adapt well to homes where children and dogs are present, and two of these cats will generally strike up quite a close bond when they are living under the same roof, especially if obtained as kittens.

FELINE CHARACTERISTICS		NOTES
Starting out	A chunky, good-looking breed, which is quite happy being left alone for periods.	
Personality	Dependable, friendly and well-balanced, as well as being affectionate.	Makes an ideal family pet.
Appearance	Large, cobby breed originally created from street cats.	A wide choice of colors and patterns.
At home	Very adaptable breed that likes to venture outdoors regularly.	Males grow larger than females, with prominent jowls on their faces.
Behavior	Quiet and not especially demonstrative by nature, but appreciates attention.	
Grooming	Occasional brushing will keep its dense, plush coat in good condition.	Groom more frequently when the cat is shedding, to guard against fur balls.
Common health issues	Occasional cases of hypertrophic cardiomyopathy (HCM) recorded in this breed.	Believed to be an inherited problem.

Face shape
Large, rounded face with relatively small ears.

Coat
Dense, plush texture that needs little grooming to look immaculate.

Color
This is a blue example of the breed, representing one of the traditional colors.

4. Exotic Shorthair

The Exotic came about as a result of deliberate crossbreeding between British Shorthairs and Persian Longhairs. It is essentially a breed possessing the temperament of both of these breeds, but it does not require the same amount of grooming as a Persian Longhair.

History

The original aim of mating these two breeds was to boost the size of the British Shorthair, but in terms of their physical appearance, or "type," many of the resulting kittens were unsuitable to show as British Shorthairs. Their facial shape was too similar to that of a Persian, or their coat was often too long or differed in texture from that of a British Shorthair. There was no denying their appeal, though, especially to would-be owners who felt unable to cope with the coat care necessary for a Persian. Since then, the cats have built up a strong following, initially in North America and now worldwide, not just because of their appearance, but also because of their good temperament and home-loving nature.

Coat

The texture of the Exotic's coat is soft, reflecting its Persian Longhair ancestry, while its dense, plush nature is a characteristic associated with the British Shorthair. The overall coat length of these cats is longer than that of a traditional shorthair and yet should not be so long that it flows, as with a longhaired cat. Exotics have now been bred in many varieties, including not just self-colored (solids) but also tabbies (as shown here), smokes, and bicolors.

Facial features
Flattened face and stubby nose are reflections of their Persian ancestry.

FELINE CHARACTERISTICS		NOTES
Starting out	Cute appearance, with these cats effectively being a shorter-haired Persian.	Created from British Shorthairs in the U.K.
Personality	Relaxed, quiet, and good-natured, enjoys being stroked and fussed over.	
Appearance	Flattened facial profile like a Persian, but the coat is relatively short.	
At home	Home-loving and displays little desire to hunt if allowed outdoors.	
Behavior	Makes an excellent household pet, due to its very friendly nature.	
Grooming	Needs far less grooming than a Persian, but this must not be neglected.	Coat is more profuse than in the case of a typical shorthair.
Common health issues	Can suffer from tear stains, caused by malformed tear ducts.	This causes staining on the coat at the corners of the eyes near the nose.

Tail
This is relatively short and thick.

Limbs
Short, powerful legs with large, rounded paws.

5. Burmilla

This particular breed is distinguished as being the first ever created with "sound temperament" required as part of its official judging standard. Burmillas are very attractive cats, and unsurprisingly, they make excellent companions.

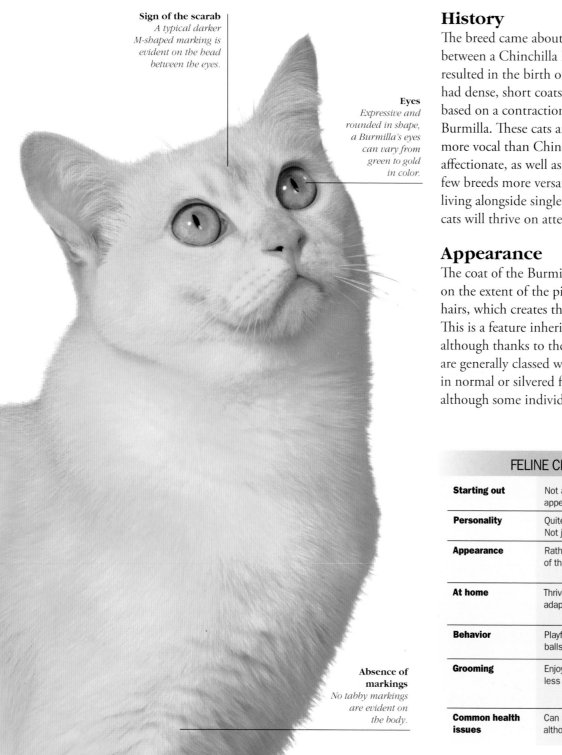

Sign of the scarab
A typical darker M-shaped marking is evident on the head between the eyes.

Eyes
Expressive and rounded in shape, a Burmilla's eyes can vary from green to gold in color.

Absence of markings
No tabby markings are evident on the body.

History

The breed came about by chance, as the result of an unplanned mating between a Chinchilla Persian and a lilac Burmese in 1981. This resulted in the birth of four black, shaded silver kittens, all of which had dense, short coats. The breed name that ultimately resulted was based on a contraction of Burmese and Chinchilla, thereby creating Burmilla. These cats are less lively than true Burmese and rather more vocal than Chinchilla Persians. Burmillas are playful and very affectionate, as well as being surprisingly gentle by nature. There are few breeds more versatile as companions, being well suited either to living alongside single people of any age or as part of a family. These cats will thrive on attention and form a close bond with people.

Appearance

The coat of the Burmilla can be either shaded or tipped, depending on the extent of the pigmentation extending down the individual hairs, which creates the breed's distinctive shimmering appearance. This is a feature inherited from its Chinchilla Persian ancestor, although thanks to their Burmese ancestry and short coats, these cats are generally classed within the Asian group. They can be bred either in normal or silvered forms. Grooming care is straightforward, although some individuals have plusher coats than others.

FELINE CHARACTERISTICS		NOTES
Starting out	Not always easy to predict the likely adult appearance in the case of kittens.	
Personality	Quite relaxed, more so than a Burmese. Not just a lap cat though.	
Appearance	Rather sophisticated and unusual in terms of the breed's markings.	The Burmilla's patterning is individual as well.
At home	Thrives on company. Learns quickly and adapts to routines.	Makes an excellent companion, especially if owner is home all day.
Behavior	Playful side to its nature, especially chasing balls, and enjoys attention.	Curious as well. Likes to investigate.
Grooming	Enjoys being groomed, but this activity is less essential than with many breeds.	
Common health issues	Can suffer from polycystic kidneys, although this is not a widespread problem.	

6. American Ringtail

Changes in tail length are to be seen in various breeds, but the significant factor in the case of these cats is the actual shape of the tail, which is typically kept curled. American Ringtails are rare at present.

History

Their origins can be traced back to a shorthaired kitten that was found in 1998 as a stray in northern California's San Francisco Bay area. Hand-reared by its rescuer, Susan Manley, this particular young cat named Solomon grew up with a very unusual appearance, because of his tail. About a third of its length extending from the base was upright, and then it fell forward in a loose curl over the back. Solomon's patterning was similar to that of a Birman, with white fur on the front paws and a more extensive white area extending up the hind legs. His overall coloration was blue, with faint tabby markings on the tail, and a white patch on the chest. Solomon's first litter was born in January 2004, after ongoing veterinary checks to ensure that he was healthy.

Tail talk

Veterinary investigations into Solomon's unusual tail revealed that he was not suffering from any abnormality of the vertebral column. In fact, he was quite healthy, with the tail not being set in a curled position. He was able to extend his tail if he wanted to do so, and its flexibility resulted from the presence of more highly developed muscles at its base. This is the reason that the base of the tail is thicker than in the case of other breeds.

FELINE CHARACTERISTICS		NOTES
Starting out	Distinguished not by the pattern on its tail, but by the way the tail is carried.	Very rare at present. Originated on the West coast.
Personality	Affectionate and friendly, mirroring its ordinary domestic cat origins.	Crosses with the Ragdoll should ensure a very relaxed nature.
Appearance	Tail resembles a ring at its tip. Now being developed in a longhaired form, too.	
At home	Undemanding, with recent Ragdoll input making these cats more home-loving.	
Behavior	Playful and likes to be involved in family life. Quite adaptable by nature.	
Grooming	Shorthaired form needs minimal grooming, but longhairs will require more.	
Common health issues	None recoded to date. The spinal column and hips are quite healthy in this case.	

Head shape
The length of the American Ringtail's head is slightly longer than its width.

Flexible tail
Hangs down but is never tightly curled over the back, and the cat can actually move it freely. Curling is the result of a recessive gene.

Increased size
Crosses with the Ragdoll breeds have now led to an increase in the size of these cats.

7. Ragdoll

When it comes to friendly lap cats, the Ragdoll is one of the most popular. First bred in California, it is now widely kept in many countries. Its placid nature extends outdoors, too, with Ragdolls not inclined to hunt wildlife.

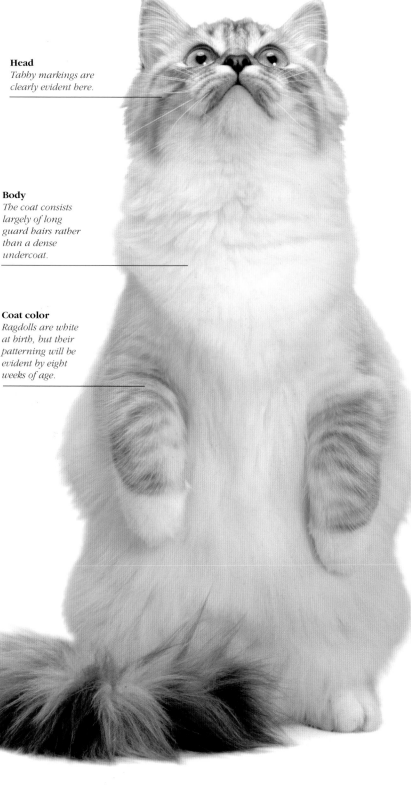

Head
Tabby markings are clearly evident here.

Body
The coat consists largely of long guard hairs rather than a dense undercoat.

Coat color
Ragdolls are white at birth, but their patterning will be evident by eight weeks of age.

History

The first Ragdolls had a peculiar mythology attached to them. Their mother was a white longhaired cat, named Josephine, who may have been a Persian Longhair or possibly an Angora. She was involved in an accident just before giving birth, but luckily, both she and her kittens survived. All the young cats were exceptionally docile, and this led their breeder, Ann Baker, to suggest that they had lost the ability to feel any pain as a result of Josephine's accident. In spite of the fact that there was no truth whatsoever in this suggestion, this idea captured public attention and generated considerable interest in the emerging breed.

Patterning

There are three varieties—the pointed, mitted, and bicolor. The mitted form can be separated at a glance from the pointed, due to the distinctive white areas on the paws, breaking the darker coloration evident here. The abdomen is white, and there may or may not be a white blaze extending between the eyes. It is easy to distinguish these cats from Birmans, which have similar broken point coloration, simply because Ragdolls have white fur on the chin. Ragdolls mature slowly, and it can take three to four years before they are fully grown, with their coats looking their best.

FELINE CHARACTERISTICS		NOTES
Starting out	Cute, cuddly kittens that ultimately grow into large adult cats.	Will take up to 8 weeks or so to develop their characteristic coloration.
Personality	Very laid-back, placid, and friendly, and do not resent being lifted up.	Equally suited as a family pet or for people living on their own.
Appearance	Three different varieties to choose from, being bred in a range of colors.	Large breed with males weighing over 20 lbs (9.1kg).
At home	Ideal companion breed, settling well in the home and not inclined to wander.	
Behavior	No real aggressive tendencies and very home-loving.	
Grooming	Should be groomed twice a week, but coat isn't inclined to mat.	
Common health issues	Susceptible to feline hypertrophic cardiomyopathy.	

8. Ragamuffin

These cats are very closely related to the Ragdoll, having evolved from the same bloodline. They are therefore very similar in temperament, although not as well known. Being a large breed, it can be four years before they are fully grown.

History

When the Ragdoll breed came into existence, its creator, Ann Baker, trademarked this name. She also sought to prevent breeders from having their cats recognized for show purposes through the major breed registries, setting up her own registry called the International Ragdoll Cat Association (IRCA). In 1994, a group of Ragdoll breeders broke away, however, concerned about the restrictions that were placed on them. Unable to use the description of Ragdoll for their cats, they decided to rename them as Ragamuffins. As a result of widespread concerns about serious inbreeding, these enthusiasts started to outcross their cats to other breeds, which included both Persian Longhairs and Himalayans.

The breed today

One of the most evident differences today is the much wider range of colors existing in the case of the Ragamuffin, compared with Ragdolls. In fact, there are generally no color restrictions in the case of this breed, although certain varieties, such as white, are more highly sought after than others. Great emphasis has been placed on maintaining the friendly, social nature of these cats, and they will meow and purr readily, often striking up a conversation with their owners.

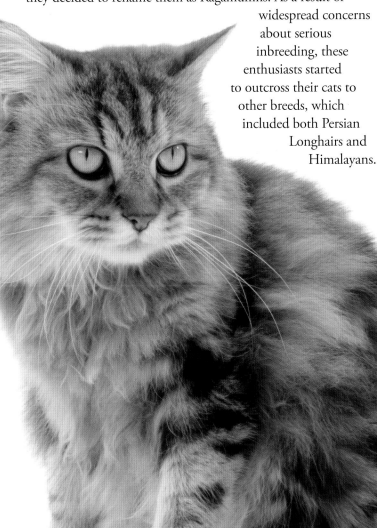

FELINE CHARACTERISTICS		NOTES
Starting out	Very friendly, gentle breed that is closely allied to the Ragdoll.	
Personality	Relaxed, very placid, and not difficult to pick up and pet, in spite of its size.	
Appearance	Bred in all colors and patterns, and an especially large breed when adult.	
At home	Ideal as a family pet, being tolerant of children and happy living with a dog.	Docile nature means it may be bullied outdoors by neighborhood cats.
Behavior	Playful but not demanding. Can prove to be quite vocal on occasions.	
Grooming	Needs to be brushed and combed two or three times a week.	Will shed winter coat in the spring, so more grooming essential.
Common health issues	Although longhaired, coat is not inclined to mat, but at risk from fur balls.	Coat texture has been likened to that of rabbits' fur.

Patterning
This is a tabby individual, as shown by its markings.

Coat
Their coats are easy to groom, with the fur tending not to mat readily.

9. Scottish Fold

Their cute appearance and friendly nature have led to Scottish Folds becoming very popular, especially in North America, where the breed was essentially developed into a show cat. This particular individual is an example of the shorthaired rather than the longhaired form.

AT A GLANCE

- Folded yet mobile ears
- Resembles British Shorthairs
- Placid, getting along well with people
- Affectionate yet quiet

History

These cats owe their origins to an unexpected mutation that appeared during 1961 in a litter of kittens born on a farm near Coupar Angus in Perthshire, Scotland. A white kitten named Susie was obtained by a shepherd named William Ross, and the ancestry of all Scottish Folds alive today ultimately traces back to her. Sadly, she was killed at an early age as the result of a collision with a car, but not before she had produced another kitten with folded ears, named Snooks, who carried on the bloodline. Scottish Folds were initially highly controversial, because of fears over deafness, which subsequently proved to be unfounded, although they may produce more ear wax than usual.

FELINE CHARACTERISTICS		NOTES
Starting out	Unmistakable appearance, bred in a wide range of colors and patterns.	Both Folds and non-Folds born in a litter will have upright ears at first.
Personality	Affectionate and adaptable, with a relatively placid nature.	
Appearance	Distinctive, having folded ears with a body type like a British Shorthair.	As with British Shorthairs, males are larger than females.
At home	Settles well in the home, but does like to explore outdoors as well.	
Behavior	Quiet by nature. Frequently likes to sleep lying on its back, not on its side.	
Grooming	Brush the coat perhaps once a week—more frequently when shedding.	
Common health issues	Folds must not be paired together, as this can cause skeletal problems.	They are paired with non-Folds.

Coat
The coat in this case is short and requires relatively little grooming.

Ears
All cats in a Scottish Fold litter have unfolded ears initially. Those that will become Scottish Folds are recognizable by about three weeks old.

Understanding the breed

It soon became clear that mating a Scottish Fold to a cat with ordinary ears would result in a percentage of Scottish Fold offspring, confirming that this is a dominant mutation. Two of these cats with folded ears must not be mated together, though, because a percentage of the offspring will be affected by joint problems. Folds are therefore mated to non-Folds. In the U.S., where they became popular, having been rejected by British breeders initially, British and American Shorthairs served as outcrosses and increased the breed's size.

Unique markings
The patterning of individuals is unique. Bicolors such as this red-and-white tabby are not uncommon.

10. Somali

This breed was highly controversial for many years. Those keeping Abyssinian cats were very reluctant to admit that longhaired individuals occasionally cropped up in litters, but today, however, the Somali has become widely accepted and popular in its own right.

AT A GLANCE

- Intelligent, responsive breed
- Longhaired Abyssinian
- A ticked tabby
- Bred in various colors

Head
There is a M-shaped tabby marking evident on the forehead.

Chin
The whisker pads are dark, contrasting with the white area of fur on the chin.

History

No one is certain when the longhaired gene entered the Abyssinian bloodline, but it may have been as a result of some crossbreeding involving the Balinese breed as far back as the 1920s. Just as in the case of the Abyssinian, the traditional color is known as the usual or the ruddy. The sorrel is lighter in color, while the blue form has oatmeal-colored underparts. In total, there are now currently 28 different Somali varieties that have been created.

Variety
The coloration and the black tip to the tail indicate that this is a usual or ruddy.

FELINE CHARACTERISTICS		NOTES
Starting out	This is the longhaired form of the Abyssinian.	
Personality	Friendly, intelligent, and playful by nature, making a great companion.	
Appearance	A ticked tabby, with the barring on the legs and necklaces missing.	The solid tabby barring has been removed by selective breeding over generations.
At home	Likes to explore, but also will prove very affectionate.	
Behavior	Quiet by nature, and agile. Can prove to be determined hunters, too.	
Grooming	Must be carried out most frequently in the spring, when the winter coat is shed.	The coat tends to be shed heavily over a short period.
Common health issues	Dental problems have been an issue and a metabolic illness—Pyruvate Kinase Deficiency (PKDef).	Cats carrying the PKDef gene can be identified by a DNA test.

Color

The distinctive appearance of the Somali results from the ticking on its individual hairs, and the longer coat length allows for more banding than in the case of the Abyssinian. There will be a minimum of 6, and potentially as many as 14, alternate bands of the base color and the top color. Various parts of the body, such as the tip of the tail, display color corresponding to that of the ticking. This feature starts to develop in kittens from three months onward.

Cat types for people who
have plenty of space in their
homes, the time to play, and
a safe area outside for their pets.

Blue-cream

Tortoiseshell

Cats with Energy

All cats are lively at times, especially as kittens. They sometimes become so excited that they rush around wildly, leaping over furniture and dashing through the home, wherever doors are open. These sudden displays of energy often occur soon after a young cat has woken up and are more likely to be seen indoors when the weather is bad, because the cat is reluctant to go outside. Out in the yard, they can also behave in a similar way, running around and leaping up trees.

This phase passes as they mature, but in the case of the cats that are the subject of this chapter, they need more opportunity to exercise than others. This means that they can be less suited to living indoors on a permanent basis. One of the key indicators that sets them apart is their relatively athletic build.

As high-energy cats, they need time spent with them, with the majority of these breeds, such as the Cornish Rex and Burmilla, being very playful. They have lively, curious natures, and so they particularly benefit from being provided with a range of toys to keep them occupied. Some cats will even choose to play by themselves at times—patting a small ball across a wooden floor and then chasing after it.

Bicolored Oriental

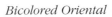

1. Burmese

This Asian breed, which occurs in parts of Myanmar (formerly known as Burma), Thailand, and Malaysia, has become very popular today, having evolved along slightly different lines in North America compared with Europe. Agile by nature and highly affectionate, Burmese make very attractive companions.

AT A GLANCE
- Very playful
- Quite vocal
- Occurs in a range of colors
- Smooth coat

History

Although they have been kept in Asia for many centuries, it was not until 1930 that the first example of the breed was imported to the U.S., having been incorrectly described there by some as a dark-colored Siamese. Dr. Thompson, who brought this cat, christened Wong Mau ('mau' means "cat"), back with him, was unconvinced, however, and set out to show by a careful breeding program that she represented a separate breed. When paired back with one of her own offspring, Wong Mau produced a new, much darker-colored kitten, which represents the traditional color associated with the Burmese breed today. The popularity of these cats increased quickly, and by the late 1950s, Burmese were already being widely kept in many countries.

Subsequent development

European bloodlines are also derived from Wong Mau, but their breeding followed a different path, with greater involvement of Siamese (see page 86) crosses in their development. This has created a type of cat with a more angular head profile, compared with the decidedly rounded appearance of North American lines, and their eyes are also more akin to those of Siamese cats. Color differences are apparent, too, because the addition of the red gene to European Burmese lines means that not just red but other varieties such as cream are also recognized.

FELINE CHARACTERISTICS		NOTES
Starting out	Cute kittens develop into highly affectionate adult cats.	Recognition of different colors and varieties.
Personality	Affectionate and eager to join in with family life. Thrives on attention.	
Appearance	Distinction now exists between European and North American Burmese.	European Burmese are shown in separate classes at North American shows.
At home	Extrovert, with a playful nature, and relatively vocal. Does not like to be ignored.	
Behavior	Quite athletic, likes to climb. Eager to play as well, chases after toys.	
Grooming	Minimal grooming needs. Stroking will help to keep the coat looking glossy.	Provide a scratching post indoors.
Common health issues	Can suffer from "cherry eye" when the tear duct becomes exposed.	Can be corrected surgically.

Eyes
These can vary from yellowish to gold in color, although blue Burmese can have greener eyes.

Coat
The traditional dark coloration of the Burmese is described as sable.

Paws
Strong and able to grasp objects well.

2. Angora

The Angora breed is not the same as the Turkish Angora (see page 134), but instead it has been created from an Oriental breeding program. These cats are therefore very athletic in build and active by nature, jumping and climbing readily.

AT A GLANCE

- Athletic nature
- Wide color choice
- Easy to groom
- Friendly nature

FELINE CHARACTERISTICS		NOTES
Starting out	A wide choice of colors and patterns from which to choose.	Coat lies sleek, emphasizing patterning present in the coat.
Personality	More placid than a Siamese, due to the Abyssinian influence.	
Appearance	A semi-longhaired cat, with the coat being longer in the winter than during the summer.	The coat has a very attractive silky texture.
At home	Settles well, and will prove to be affectionate as well as active and playful by nature.	
Behavior	Demonstrative, but not as vocal as Siamese, although they are not quiet.	
Grooming	Be prepared to groom more during periods of shedding, but not that time consuming.	
Common health issues	No significant problems have been recorded in this breed.	

History

The breed's origins date back to the 1960s, when a sorrel Abyssinian was mated to a seal-point Siamese. The aim was to create a Siamese with ticked tabby markings on the points, but the lasting impact of such crossings was to introduce the hidden longhaired gene from the Abyssinian bloodline (which gave rise to the Somali—see page 101) into Oriental breeds. A wide range of different Angora colors are recognized, not just in terms of self (solid) colors such as cinnamon, but patterned varieties, too, such as tabbies and tortoiseshells, as well as others including shaded and smokes.

The relative absence of any undercoat means that the Angora's coat does not become easily matted.

Ears
The hair in the ears, known as furnishings, is quite long.

Eye coloration
The eyes are green in all Angoras, aside from the white, which has blue eyes.

Patterning
Tabby markings are clearly evident as darker markings on the coat.

Identification issues

In common with other cats of Oriental origins, Angoras have relatively long, muscular bodies. Their fur is longer over the body itself but shorter on the face and legs. It has a fine, silky texture. There is some lingering confusion over the name of these particular cats, however, as they are described in parts of mainland Europe as Javanese. In North America, though, this description is applied to nontraditional color variants of the Balinese, which is the longhaired form of the Siamese.

3. Burmilla

The Burmese contribution to the ancestry of this particular breed helps explain its energetic nature. Yet the Chinchilla Longhair input into the bloodline has served to ensure that Burmillas are not as frenetic as many other breeds with an Oriental ancestry, even when they are kittens.

AT A GLANCE
- Great temperament
- Individual patterning
- Athletic nature
- An instinctively playful breed

History

Careful monitoring of the breeding program for the Burmilla has resulted in a very well-adjusted breed that will form a close bond with people. The energy of these cats can be channeled very easily into play, and they enjoy having access to a wide range of toys. Each tends to display individual preferences, with even littermates differing in this regard. Some may prefer balls or similar toys to chase after, whereas others like to jump up at wands. Toys that test the cat's intelligence, dispensing treats, are especially popular with this breed. Encouraging your cat to play regularly will reinforce the bond between you, as well as helping it stay healthy.

The big outdoors

Burmillas enjoy climbing, and their relatively svelte body shape assists them in this respect. As with other cats, they literally haul themselves up a tree trunk, using their claws—like a climber's crampons for anchorage and the power in the muscles of their hind legs for the ascent. When coming down the trunk, the cat will head down backward in a similar fashion, until it is close to the ground, and then it turns around and jumps, landing on its front feet.

FELINE CHARACTERISTICS

For Feline Characteristics, see page 48

Patterning
Shaded patterning on the body varies in extent, from relatively light to dark.

Tail
This is relatively short and does not taper significantly.

Eyes
Relatively large, round, green eyes.

Tabby markings
These are absent from the Burmilla's body but may be evident on the face, legs, and tail.

4. Cornish Rex

These cats have a muscular profile. Their hindquarters are especially powerful, enabling them to leap onto work surfaces or even shelves in the home with relatively little effort. They may sit in an upright position (as shown), too, similar to a dog.

AT A GLANCE
- Slim, elegant appearance
- Distinctive, easy-care coat
- Friendly personality
- Great athlete

History

It was in 1950 that a strange, curly coated kitten cropped up in a litter born to a farm cat in Cornwall, in the southwest of England. The breeder recognized this mutation as being similar to the rex variety seen in some rabbit breeds and set out to establish it. In the early stages, both Burmese and British Shorthairs were used as outcrosses, whereas in North America, where the breed was imported during 1957, Siamese and Oriental bloodlines were preferred for this purpose. This has created a lasting difference, as reflected by different breed standards on opposite sides of the Atlantic. American Cornish Rex have a more Oriental appearance, as can be seen in their angular head shape, compared with those kept in Great Britain.

FELINE CHARACTERISTICS		NOTES
Starting out	Wide range of different colors and varieties to choose from in this breed.	
Personality	Surprisingly social with other cats, and also gentle by nature.	
Appearance	Very distinctive curly coated appearance.	
At home	Not a breed to be ignored, these Rexes like plenty of attention, and a cat-friendly environment.	Keep two Cornish Rexes together as company for each other if you are out at work.
Behavior	Like to play, reflecting the active side to their nature, chasing after toys.	
Grooming	Does not shed heavily. Stroking will help emphasize the distinctive coat.	Check the ears regularly for wax, wiping the flaps with damp cotton balls.
Common health issues	Prone to obesity; keep your cat's weight under review, especially after neutering.	Follow on-pack feeding instructions, and avoid extra treats.

Ears
Large, open ears set high up on the head.

Legs
These are decidedly long and slender in shape, ending in small, oval-shaped paws.

Tail
The long, narrow tail helps the cat balance when standing on its hind legs.

The coat

The Cornish Rex lacks any long guard hairs in its coat, and as a consequence, its appearance results essentially from its undercoat. As a result, the coat is not just much shorter than normal but also has a much finer texture. It has a wavy appearance, with this feature particularly apparent over the back and on the sides of the body. The relative absence of fur does mean that these cats tend to feel the cold more than many other breeds.

5. Devon Rex

This particular breed also arose unexpectedly in the southwest of England but was soon proven to be the result of a completely separate mutation to the Cornish Rex. The two breeds of cats are similar in temperament, however, with a rather mischievous side to their natures.

AT A GLANCE
- Distinctive facial features
- Highly intelligent
- Agile climber
- Lively, active companion

FELINE CHARACTERISTICS		NOTES
Starting out	Available in a wide range of colors and patterned forms as well.	Colorpointed Devon Rexes are often called Si-rexes.
Personality	Rather doglike in various respects, and likes to chase after toys.	
Appearance	Said to resemble a pixie—thanks to the shape of its face and mischievous nature.	
At home	Lively and destined to make an impression, particularly as a youngster.	Older Devon Rexes tend to become less active.
Behavior	Highly curious and generally not nervous in home surroundings.	
Grooming	Very little grooming is needed. Simply wipe the fur with a chamois leather.	Stroking will also help keep it in good condition.
Common health issues	Can suffer from skin problems, which are often caused by a yeast infection.	

History

The origins of the Devon Rex can be traced back to a stray tom cat, with a strange, curly coat that mated with a local cat in the Devon village of Buckfastleigh, in 1960. All attempts to catch the adult male failed, but his son, called Kirlee, passed on his distinctive genes. The Devon Rex is also sometimes described as the pixie cat, which tends to emphasize the active, playful side to the breed's nature. In some ways, it behaves more like a dog than a cat, as it is incredibly responsive to training. Some young Devon Rexes can be taught to sit and walk to heel, as well as to retrieve objects. They also soon learn to come when called.

Ears
Large and incredibly wide, with tufts at their rounded tips.

Surveying their surroundings

Lively and engaging by nature, these Rexes can jump and climb very well, often preferring to sleep off the ground. A Devon Rex often delights in being provided with a hammock-style bed that can be attached over a radiator, helping it keep warm on cold days, when its thin coat offers less protection against the elements. They retain their playful instincts throughout their lives and delight in the company of people, which has helped ensure their popularity.

Markings
Darker tabby markings are most evident on the legs and tail, rather than on the body.

Coat
The short guard hairs are mixed with down in the coat, which feels soft to the touch.

6. Egyptian Mau

This particular breed has a long history, with some people believing that its origins trace back directly to the cats of ancient Egypt. It is still a relatively scarce breed today, especially in Europe, although it is better known in North America.

AT A GLANCE

- Possibly the oldest surviving cat breed
- Characteristic spotted tabby coat
- Occurs in three varieties
- Randomly distributed markings

History

The ancestors of the modern breed were discovered on the streets of Cairo, Egypt, by a Russian émigré named Nathalie Troubetskoy. There are three traditional colors associated with the breed. These are the silver (seen here), the bronze, which is actually a coppery shade with dark markings, and the smoke. In fact, the Egyptian Mau is the only cat that has a patterned smoke form as a recognized variety, displaying the characteristic spotted tabby markings associated with the breed. Occasionally, classic (blotched) tabby forms of the Egyptian Mau are recorded in litters, but these cats cannot be exhibited.

What to expect

Few cats are more active than Egyptian Maus, thriving on close interaction with their owners, and they are generally always willing to play games from an early age, even acting as retrievers. Their reflexes are incredibly fast. Members of this breed form a close bond with people in their immediate circle and can learn from example by watching their owners. This, in turn, may allow them to open the doors to cupboards and even drawers around the home. Be especially careful with a refrigerator. If you feed your cat treats from here, you are likely to find that your pet starts helping itself if you leave the door open and turn away, even for a brief moment!

Feet
Small, oval-shaped paws.

Necklaces
These are the broken black stripes encircling the neck.

Eye markings
So-called black mascara lines help accentuate the facial features.

FELINE CHARACTERISTICS		NOTES
Starting out	A strikingly marked cat, with the appearance of kittens not changing as they mature.	The patterning of each of these cats is individual.
Personality	Lively, active nature, as befits their street cat origins.	
Appearance	Breed distinguished by its spotted tabby appearance and the green color of its eyes.	Bred in three distinct colors.
At home	Appreciates a range of toys in the home and will use an activity center, too.	
Behavior	Will prove to be very lively and needs plenty of attention.	
Grooming	Minimal grooming needs, with gentle brushing usually sufficing for this purpose.	
Common health issues	No particular health problems have been reported in these cats.	Regular health checks recommended for older individuals.

7. Nebelung

The Nebelung is a modern recreation of one of the early breeds seen at the cat shows of the late 1800s. It has an energetic nature, but perhaps surprisingly, it is also a breed that can settle well in indoor surroundings.

AT A GLANCE
- Sparkling coat
- Intelligent nature
- Aloof with strangers
- Happy as part of a family

History

This particular breed came about as the result of a breeding program to recreate the Russian Blue longhair that had disappeared in the twentieth century. The breeding program began in the U.S. during the mid-1980s, involving blue cats with medium-length coats that shimmered and sparkled with a silvery sheen. The Nebelung's unusual name stems from the German word, which translates as "mist creature," and refers to the breed's coloration. The relatively powerful body of these cats is in keeping with their athletic appearance. The body is relatively long, with the fur longest over the tail, creating a distinct brush here. Male Nebelungs, in particular, may develop a ruff of longer fur around the neck, especially in the winter.

FELINE CHARACTERISTICS		NOTES
Starting out	Not a wide choice of colors. This reflects the breed's Russian ancestry.	Aside from the blue shown here, there is also a less common white variety.
Personality	Can be slightly shier than many breeds but forms a strong bond with its owners.	
Appearance	Silver tipping on the guard hairs underlies the breed's sparkling appearance.	
At home	Makes a gentle, affectionate companion. Calm by nature and quiet.	Not a breed that will thrive in the company of boisterous dogs.
Behavior	Not prone to roaming but quite active and agile in the home. Enjoys playing.	
Grooming	This needs to be carried out regularly, especially during the winter months.	Double-layered but semi-longhaired soft coat.
Common health issues	No particular health problems have been reported in these cats.	

Head
This is wedge-shaped rather than rounded.

Neck
A surprisingly long and graceful neck.

Appearance

The breed standard for the Nebelung, which is starting to gain international show recognition, is similar to that of the Russian itself (see page 98). The eyes are oval in shape and green in color, being yellowish in kittens. The ears appear large, particularly at the base and have slightly rounded tips. In terms of physique, however, Nebelungs should resemble Russians, with silvery hairs among the blue serving to match their coloring. Nebelungs have proved to be quite fussy cats, especially with regard to food. They also do not take to strangers readily.

Coat
Distinguished by relatively long, silky hair that will need to be brushed about twice a week.

8. Oriental

There are more potential varieties in the case of the Oriental than in any other breed, with literally hundreds of possibilities to choose from. Some theoretical combinations have not even been created yet. Orientals are demonstrative, vocal, and lively cats.

AT A GLANCE
- Affectionate nature
- Attention-seeking
- Playful and lively
- Many colors and varieties

History

In the early days of the Siamese, at the turn of the twentieth century, there were both colorpointed Siamese cats and self-colored (solid) cats of corresponding type. By the 1920s, however, these self-colored cats had basically disappeared, once it was decreed that only blue-eyed Siamese could be exhibited. The Orientals are a recreation of that lost bloodline, so that, literally, they are cats that resemble Siamese in terms of their type but do not display their characteristic pointed appearance. Their revival began during the 1950s, and today they have a worldwide following. Unsurprisingly perhaps, they are very similar to Siamese in temperament, too, which means that they are very active cats. They climb well and have an assertive personality, which means that they are not easily overlooked, even in a busy household. Orientals are instinctive extroverts, with a very playful side to their character.

Color

Self-colored (solid) Orientals predominated at first, but since those early days, a huge number of color varieties have since been developed. There are tortoiseshell and tabby forms, with patterning showing up very clearly, thanks to their short, sleek coats. Smoke, shaded, and tipped varieties also exist. Bicolors like this individual are a relatively recent development, but they have already gained recognition for show purposes in North America.

Ears
Large, pricked ears continue the line of the head.

Feet
Paws can be used for patting, to obtain attention, and for pouncing.

Pattern
The contrast between the colored and white areas should be clearly defined.

FELINE CHARACTERISTICS		NOTES
Starting out	Huge choice, in terms of colors and patterns, but some are bred more widely.	Self-colored (solid) varieties still have a widespread following.
Personality	Highly demonstrative, lively, and vocal. A breed that demands attention.	
Appearance	Sleek, good-looking, elegant cats with an angular head.	
At home	Must have plenty of attention if it is not to become bored.	Toys should always be provided, and set aside time to play with your cat.
Behavior	People-centric cats that are keen to engage with members of their immediate family.	
Grooming	Short coat needs very little grooming, although these cats do enjoy the process.	Regular stroking will be effective to remove loose hair from the coat.
Common health issues	Respiratory infections and, occasionally, also inherited heart problems.	

9. Pixiebob

These cats are highly individual and possess a rather independent side to their nature, as their distinctive, wild-looking appearance suggests. This is not a breed that takes well to being confined indoors on a permanent basis, possibly because of its free-roaming origins.

AT A GLANCE

- Distinctive appearance
- High-energy breed
- Friendly nature
- Sharp hunting instincts

History

Individual stray or even feral cats without tails have been recorded in rural areas of the U.S. for some time. In some cases, it may be that the cat simply lost its tail in an accident rather than for any genetic reason. The story developed, however, that such cats were actually hybrids, being the result of mating between farm cats or strays and the Bobcat (*Lynx rufus*). Although now disproved by DNA analysis, this belief still lingers in some areas. The origins of the Pixiebob as a breed extend back to 1985, when a breeder named Carol Anne Brewer obtained two stray kittens of this type and, in due course, bred another with a short tail that she dubbed Pixie.

Progress

Pixie's name is now commemorated in that of the breed, which remains scarce outside North America, although it was introduced to Europe in 2001. The coloration of these cats is basically that of a brown tabby, with nonpedigree cats displaying this patterning, having been used as outcrosses. Many of the original cats that contributed to the breed's development were strays. An unusual breed characteristic is that these cats tend to communicate by a series of chirping calls, rather than meowing.

FELINE CHARACTERISTICS		NOTES
Starting out	Distinctive "wild cat" look, but a strictly domestic breed created from strays.	Modeled on the appearance of the North American Bobcat.
Personality	Alert, attentive, quiet by nature, and playful, even learning to retrieve toys.	
Appearance	Has a distinctive look of a wild cat, with a characteristic bobtail.	This mutation has cropped up in domestic cats in various parts of the world.
At home	Lively and active, being very loyal to members of the immediate family.	Quite happy living with dogs.
Behavior	Intelligent companion and adaptable by nature, settling well in the home.	
Grooming	Relatively minimal grooming required, in spite of the double-layered coat.	
Common health issues	Often polydactyl, with extra toes on its feet, but this causes no handicap.	

Tail
The short tail is described as a bobtail. Some kittens in a litter will be born with full-length tails.

Color and coat
There is always white fur on the chin. Most Pixiebobs are shorthaired, but longhairs do crop up.

Size
Significantly larger than the average domestic cat, which reinforced rumors about their Bobcat ancestry.

10. Tonkinese

The pointed appearance of this cat reveals its close association with the Siamese, and its temperament is very similar. Extrovert by nature, the Tonkinese is a lively, vocal breed that craves human attention, forming a strong bond with the people in its household.

AT A GLANCE

- Lively, playful nature
- Thrives on human company
- Active nature
- Easy-care coat

History

By definition, a breed has to "breed true," which means that kittens should correspond to their parents. This does not occur in the case of Tonkinese, which makes them controversial. Instead, the likelihood is that some of the kittens in a Tonkinese litter will be Siamese-type cats, while others will be Burmese, cropping up alongside their Tonkinese littermates. Confusion in this area extends right back to when such cats first became known in the West. It has been suggested that the first recorded chocolate Siamese brought to Europe in the 1880s were probably Burmese, and the breeding records attached to Wong Mau (see page 56) definitely confirm that she was a Tonkinese, rather than a pure Burmese. What happened subsequently, however, is that breeders concentrated on producing the darkest variant, which was the Burmese, and so the attributes of the Tonkinese were lost.

Head
The shape of the head is more moderate and less triangular than that of the Siamese.

Coloration
Point coloration is still clearly discernible in the case of the Tonkinese.

Tail
Relatively long tail that must not be kinked along its length.

FELINE CHARACTERISTICS		NOTES
Starting out	Occurs in a range of different colors and patterns.	These are described in general as mink variants in North America.
Personality	A sociable, inquisitive breed that thrives on affection.	
Appearance	Effectively a mix of Siamese and Burmese, with their distinctive "aqua" eye color.	The Tonkinese tends to be intermediate in all respects.
At home	Playful nature means that these cats require plenty of attention and toys.	
Behavior	Not as vocal as Siamese themselves.	
Grooming	Regular stroking is usually quite adequate, even for removing loose hairs.	
Common health issues	Can be more vulnerable to respiratory infections, and individuals can react badly to anesthetics.	Applies to all members of the Oriental (Asian) group of cats.

Subsequent breeding

Such cats were later recreated by crossings between Burmese and Siamese in Canada, but the Tonkinese still remains rather controversial today. It has a distinctive appearance, though, described as mink. The body color is darker in this case than that of the corresponding Siamese variety, blending in well with the points. Their coloration tends to darken with age. In terms of temperament, Tonkinese are not as demanding as Siamese but still prove to be quite vocal. They tend to get along well together.

Dilute Torbie Longhair

Black-and-white Bicolor Longhair

Large Cats

It might be thought that large breeds of cats are more active than their smaller counterparts, but this is not always the case. In fact, many large breeds are quite placid, notably those that owe their origins to crosses involving the Persian, which is an especially docile breed. This explains why cats such as the Himalayan and Ragdoll are more interested in curling up by the fire than wandering off to hunt.

On the other hand, the rules of nature also come into play. Zoologists recognize what is known as Bergmann's Rule, which states that animals that have evolved in a cold climate tend to be larger than those occurring close to the Equator, where it is warmer. Although domestic cats are obviously a relatively recent addition to the list of animals on the planet, this rule applies to them.

Unlike the situation with dogs, however, there is no link between body size and lifespan, with large cats potentially living just as long as their smaller relatives. Nevertheless, it is important to bear in mind that their size means they will have correspondingly bigger appetites and so will be more expensive to keep.

Cream-and-white Selkirk Rex

1. American Bobtail

The tails of American Bobtails measure between one half and one third of those of ordinary cats, and the aim has been to create a breed with a distinctively wild appearance. The large size of these cats also emphasizes their considerable presence.

AT A GLANCE
- Wild look
- Friendly nature
- Bred in many colors
- Very active

History

This breed traces its origins back to a kitten found on a Native American reservation in Arizona by John and Brenda Sanders from Iowa. They took the abandoned young cat home and cared for him, ultimately mating him to Siamese stock, with a view to creating a bobtailed breed with the appearance of the Snowshoe (see page 99). This was unsuccessful, however, and breeders have since focused on creating a large domestic cat with a wild appearance, although there is no evidence to suggest that a Bobcat (*Lynx rufus*) was involved in its development at the outset. The majority of these cats tend to be shorthaired, which helps allow the tabby patterning that is common in this breed, but semi-longhaired individuals do also crop up quite regularly.

Patterning
The outline of spotted tabby patterning can be seen on the coat of this individual.

The tail

This is a completely separate breed to the Japanese Bobtail (see page 130), as has been proved by genetics. Whereas the Japanese breed's tail is the result of a recessive trait, which means that mating one of these cats to a cat with an ordinary tail will not produce further bobtails in the first generation, the mutation that has given rise to the American Bobtail is dominant. As a result, pairing one of these bobtails with an ordinary cat should result in a percentage of the kittens having shortened tails, too.

Noticeable barring
More prominent tabby barring is evident here.

Body size
Like other large breeds, American Bobtails develop quite slowly and will take two or three years to attain their full size.

FELINE CHARACTERISTICS		NOTES
Starting out	Highly unusual breed.	Only being bred in North America at present.
Personality	Wild cat appearance but with a domestic cat personality.	
Appearance	Relative lack of a tail is an obvious feature, and characteristic of the breed.	Tabby patterning reinforces the "wild" look of these cats.
At home	Intelligent companions, with a confident temperament in most cases.	Playful and can be rather doglike in terms of retrieving toys.
Behavior	Active and energetic nature, tolerant of handling.	
Grooming	Longhaired form needs more grooming, but coat is not difficult to maintain.	
Common health issues	Occasionally, individuals may be born without tails, with shortened spines.	

2. Cymric

This is another breed where the tail is a distinctive characteristic, and in this case, it may be absent altogether. The Cymric is the longhaired form of the well-known Manx breed (see page 132), although it is not as commonly seen.

(see page 132)

AT A GLANCE

- Various colors
- May not be tail-less
- Breeding unpredictable
- Relatively rare

FELINE CHARACTERISTICS		NOTES
Starting out	A rare, relatively hard-to-find breed. Most common in North America.	This is the longhaired form of the better-known Manx.
Personality	Well balanced, intelligent, and generally a long-lived breed.	
Appearance	Variable tail length. Can vary from long to absent.	Only the tail-less form is accepted for exhibition purposes.
At home	Playful and learn quickly, forming a strong bond with its owners.	
Behavior	Can jump well and is often fascinated by dripping faucets.	Gets along well with dogs.
Grooming	Regular grooming important, especially in the spring when the cat is shedding the most.	
Common health issues	Can suffer a variety of problems linked to the shortening of the spine.	

History

The Cymric, whose name comes from the native Welsh name for Wales—Cymru—actually originated in Canada. It was not unusual for occasional longhaired kittens to turn up in litters of Manx cats, and a group of North American breeders then decided to work together to develop this form of the Manx. As a result, it is also known as the Longhaired Manx. Just as in the case of the Manx itself, the tail length can vary, or there may be no tail at all. Cymrics with the longest tails, roughly equivalent to those of a typical domestic cat, are described as "longies," which distinguishes them from the "stumpies," which have only a very short tail.

Backline
The rump in the Cymric is unusually positioned higher than the shoulders.

Body coloration
Solid black coloration broken by a clearly defined white area—a blaze— is shown here.

Breeding

Longies are crossed with tail-less Cymrics, and a mix of these, including stumpies, may be anticipated in the litter, but only tail-less Cymrics can be exhibited, so breeding Cymrics for exhibition purposes can therefore be very frustrating, especially as they only produce small litters, and there is no guarantee than any tail-less individuals will result from a particular pairing. Nevertheless, they are friendly cats, and their coat is not especially profuse, so grooming is relatively straightforward. There are no restrictions in terms of coloration in this breed.

Big feet
It has large, powerful paws and well-boned legs.

3. Himalayan

The longhaired breed is named after the Himalayan rabbit, which displays a similar arrangement of coloring. This causes the body extremities, or "points"—the face, ears, feet, legs, and tail—to be darker in color than the rest of the body.

Little ears
These are small and tend to be partially concealed by the fur on the head.

Coat length
Long coat with a silky texture corresponds to that of a Persian and will need daily grooming.

Brushlike tail
The length of the coat here creates a brushlike effect.

FELINE CHARACTERISTICS		NOTES
Starting out	A cat that looks like a Persian.	
Personality	Gentle, calm, and friendly by nature.	
Appearance	A profuse, pale coat and dark points are characteristic of this breed.	Kittens are white at birth, starting to develop their coloration soon afterward.
At home	Enjoys attention and displays a playful side to its nature, patting balls around.	More active than actual Persians, because of the Siamese in their ancestry.
Behavior	Home-loving. May be bullied out in the neighborhood.	Makes a good house cat.
Grooming	Must be carried out daily. Helps build a bond between the cat and owner.	
Common health issues	Flattened face can lead to tear staining because of blockage of the tear ducts.	Those with longer muzzles are less likely to be afflicted by this problem.

History

The development of the Himalayan came about as the result of genetic investigations carried out during the 1920s and 1930s. The aim was to see if Siamese patterning could be transferred to another breed, with the Persian Longhair being chosen for this purpose. In the U.S., a black Persian was used initially, and all the kittens were of this color, but when these were mated back to Siamese, the first examples of the Himalayan Longhair resulted. Outside of North America, this breed is better known as the Colorpoint Longhair, although originally, the results of such crosses were described as Khmers. These cats display not just the points, but also the distinctive Siamese blue-eye coloration.

Color development

The development of the points depends on the cat's body temperature. Kittens are white at birth and then start to develop their point coloration soon afterward. The color on the face forms a mask, which is usually larger in the case of the male but should not extend further over the head. Corresponding shading normally develops on the sides of the body as the cat grows older, reflecting the fact that its circulation is not as effective as when it was younger.

4. Maine Coon

Ranking as one of the largest domestic cats in the world, the Maine Coon is a breed that was developed in the U.S., and has now become one of the most popular pedigree cats worldwide, both among pet-seekers and exhibitors.

AT A GLANCE

- Unusual trilling call
- Magnificent coat
- Friendly, adaptable nature
- Wide choice of colors

History

The name of the breed commemorates the state of Maine, where the ancestors of the Maine Coon arrived by ship from Europe and possibly from farther afield. Immigrants in the 1800s brought cats with them, and gradually, a discernible longhaired breed developed, with a weather-resistant coat. These cats were working animals, too, helping protect food crops from vermin. They were a common sight at the early agricultural shows but fell out of favor as the U.S. became more urbanized.

FELINE CHARACTERISTICS		NOTES
Starting out	One of the largest of all breeds, which takes several years to mature.	The first cat breed created in the U.S. in the early 1800s.
Personality	Active, engaging, and friendly.	
Appearance	Heavily built, longhaired breed, with a distinctive, rectangular profile.	Occurs in many colors, but tabby-and-white patterning is common.
At home	Affectionate, but needs space to roam outdoors. Not suitable as a house cat.	
Behavior	Has an independent side to its nature and reasonably strong hunting instincts.	
Grooming	Must be carried out regularly, especially over the winter when the coat is at its longest.	Loose fur needs removing to guard against fur balls.
Common health issues	Can be vulnerable to hip dysplasia, causing pain and lameness.	Similar to the condition seen in dogs. The only cat that is generally affected.

Changing times

At that stage, fashion dictated that more exotic breeds, such as the Persian, were in demand, rather than a humble farm cat. It was not until the 1950s that the popularity of the Maine Coon started to revive, and since then, its numbers have grown consistently. Tabby patterning is common in the breed, as are the tufts of long hair on the ears. Male kittens will grow to a larger size than females, developing a particularly magnificent ruff around the neck in the winter. Although these cats are longhaired, the coat itself is not especially prone to matting.

Body coloration
There are few restrictions on coat coloration or patterning, but tabbies are commonly seen.

Impressive tail
A long, flowing tail, sometimes with patterning matching that of a raccoon, gives further insight into the breed's name.

5. Norwegian Forest Cat

The origins of the Norwegian Forest Cat lie virtually within the Arctic Circle, and it was originally popular as a farm cat. Often referred to simply as the "Wegie," it has a particularly dense winter coat that affords good protection against the elements.

AT A GLANCE
- A natural breed
- Loyal companion
- Somewhat free-spirited
- Likes to roam

History

Cats have been kept in Norway for more than 1,000 years, and during this period, the ancestors of today's Norwegian Forest Cats evolved in keeping with the landscape. They are athletic cats, in spite of their size, and able to climb well. Their agility has even allowed them to catch fish in streams in their native country. It was not until the 1970s that serious attempts were made to standardize these cats into a breed, and then they were first seen in the U.S. in 1979. Even today, they still display many of the characteristics of their ancestors, in behavioral terms. They like to roam, which means that they are not suited to urbanized living, and they are shy with strangers.

Characteristics

Unusually, under the breed standard, no points are awarded for the color of these cats. Instead, the emphasis is placed firmly on maintaining their physical appearance, or "type," and their distinctive coat. This has helped ensure that random outcrosses to create new colors have not been encouraged, and the breed's appearance is still largely unchanged. Unsurprisingly, the same patterns associated with ordinary domestic cats are common in the case of the Norwegian Forest Cat, too.

FELINE CHARACTERISTICS		NOTES
Starting out	An ancient breed that evolved under natural conditions.	First attracted the attention of breeders during the 1930s.
Personality	Independent but enjoys human company.	
Appearance	Large breed, with a thick, rather fluffy coat. Males larger in size than females.	
At home	Something of an outdoor cat but forms a close bond with members of its family.	Its weather-resistant coat means it is well insulated against rain and snow.
Behavior	Alert, playful, and friendly companion. Does retain hunting tendencies.	
Grooming	Needs to be carried out more frequently over the winter, when the coat is more profuse.	
Common health issues	Some bloodlines affected by Glycogen Storage Disease Type IV.	Breeding stock can be screened by a DNA test for this metabolic disease.

Long tail
The long, bushy tail is approximately the same length as the body.

Blaze
A white blaze of fur between the eyes is common.

Body color
Tabby-and-white individuals are common, but self (solid) colors do occur.

6. Persian

One of the most unmistakable of all cat breeds, thanks to its long, flowing coat, the origins of the Persian reside in Asia. These cats are now widely bred and particularly popular in show circles but require a considerable amount of daily grooming.

AT A GLANCE

- High-maintenance cats
- Many colors
- Affectionate and quiet
- Tends not to stray

History

The first Persians seen in Europe were highly prized, thanks to their relatively long, white coats. The earliest examples were brought from Persia (now Iran) to Italy and from Turkey to France in the early 1600s. Portrayals of Persians through to the modern era of cat showing reveal that they have changed relatively little in appearance. Today's Persians have far more profuse coats and larger heads, but the most striking change has been the flattening out of the face, and the evident compression of the nasal area. This can result in potential breathing difficulties and can also cause Persians to have problems eating. They actually feed in a different way than other cats, scooping up pieces of kibble using the underside of their tongue.

Coloration

Self (solid) colors are traditional, but a wide range of other Persian varieties now exist, including different varieties of cameos. New colors such as chocolate have also been introduced into Persian bloodlines. Tabbies occur, too, but because of the length of the coat, their patterning is not well defined overall.

Big eyes
Large, round, coppery-orange eyes add to the Persian's appeal.

Strong markings
White hairs should not protrude into black areas of the coat and vice versa.

Thick tail
This is relatively short and thick, not tapering significantly along its length.

Sturdy limbs
Short, thick legs and stout paws.

FELINE CHARACTERISTICS		NOTES
Starting out	A large, glamorous cat with relatively short legs and a rounded face.	
Personality	Relaxed, friendly, and affectionate.	
Appearance	A large, well-built cat with a very profuse coat and a flattened face.	Available in a very wide range of colors and patterned varieties.
At home	Home-loving, suitable as a house cat, preferring tranquil surroundings.	Ideal for people living on their own.
Behavior	Displays very little instinct to hunt, and not especially active by nature.	
Grooming	This needs to be carried out every day, so as to prevent the coat from becoming matted.	Persians are the most demanding of all breeds, in terms of grooming.
Common health issues	Vulnerable to polycystic kidney disease (PKD), a progressive disease appearing later in life.	A DNA test now exists, so screening of breeding stock is possible.

7. Ragdoll

This breed has been likened to a gentle giant, on account of its size and the way in which it behaves. The Ragdoll has a very placid nature, stemming from its ancestry, although it was not originally bred for this feature.

Facial features
The muzzle is rounded, as are the blue eyes. The tips of the ears are also rounded.

Muscular body
The Ragdoll has a deep chest and a muscular body.

Matching tail
In the case of the bicolor variety, the tail should match the color of the upper body.

AT A GLANCE
- A feline heavyweight
- Occurs in Siamese-type colors
- Very friendly
- Slow to mature

History
The Ragdoll's early ancestry is somewhat unclear, but it seems likely that the Oriental colors were introduced by crossbreeding involving Birmans (see page 45). In the case of the bicolor variety shown here, there should ideally be a clear division in appearance between the upper part of the body and the underparts. There needs to be a white blaze, in the form of an inverted "V," extending down from between the eyes and broadening out over the cat's chin. The chest and underparts should be entirely white, along with the front legs. It is actually very demanding to breed good examples, with unbroken coloration along the back to the tail, extending down to the level of the upper part of the hind legs.

Problems
The distribution of white areas is the complicating factor. They may break up the colored areas of the coat in an unwanted way, as illustrated by the white stripe extending over the back, as in the case of the individual shown here. In other cases, although there may be a continuous band of color along the back to the tail, this may also contain an odd white patch or two.

FELINE CHARACTERISTICS

For Feline Characteristics, see page 50

8. Selkirk Rex

This American Rex breed is unusual, as its appearance will change markedly during its first year. Both shorthaired and longhaired examples are known, and in spite of its unusual, distinctive coat, the grooming needs of the Selkirk Rex are quite modest.

AT A GLANCE

- Attractive, cuddly appearance
- Straightforward coat care
- Wide range of colors
- Friendly nature

FELINE CHARACTERISTICS		NOTES
Starting out	Large, curly coated cat, available in a wide range of colors and patterns.	Some individuals may have a more tightly curled coat than others.
Personality	Laid-back, affectionate, but can prove rather withdrawn toward strangers.	
Appearance	Thick, plush coat—not relatively sparse like that of most Rexes.	Both longhaired and shorthaired varieties are recognized.
At home	Settles well as a companion, hardy, and will like to venture outdoors.	
Behavior	Influences of the Persian and British Shorthair, which contributed to its development, can be seen.	
Grooming	Relatively little required, although the longhaired form needs more grooming.	
Common health issues	Watch for excessive wax in the ears, triggered by curled hair present here.	This is a common feature in other Rexes.

History

The founder of the breed was a kitten born in an animal shelter in the state of Montana, the only member of the litter to display the characteristic curly coat and whiskers that typify Rex cats. In due course, when she was mated, half of her resulting kittens also displayed the Rex characteristic. This confirmed that unlike all other rex breeds, the Selkirk is a dominant mutation. Subsequent crosses helped boost its size, so the breed now has a body type similar to that of a British Shorthair.

Coat development

Having shown the typical signs of a dense, plush coat as a kitten, a young Selkirk Rex then loses this feature for months while it molts. The impact of the Rex mutation is most apparent in longhaired individuals, where the curl can develop to a greater extent. This feature is less conspicuous over the back and is instead most evident on the flanks and underparts, including the throat area. Coloration makes no difference to the degree of the curl, but where there is natural contrast between the guard hairs and undercoat, as in the case of the smoke variety, so the impact is most marked.

Similar to a fleece
The rex effect is clearly apparent here and creates what looks rather like a sheep's fleece.

Shorter tail
Rexing also extends along the tail, which is relatively short and does not taper substantially along its length.

9. Siberian

This breed has only become more widely known since the breakup of the former U.S.S.R. in the late 1980s. Up until then, it was barely ever seen outside Russia, where its ancestors had roamed the far north for more than 1,000 years.

AT A GLANCE

- Historical breed
- Inquisitive nature
- Patterned varieties are common
- Variable grooming needs

History

The Siberian was originally called the Siberian Forest Cat when it became known in the West. Later its name was shortened. These cats bear an obvious resemblance to the Norwegian Forest Cat (see page 72), but this is a matter of what could be termed "convergent evolution," rather than a close direct relationship, as their homelands are separated by thousands of miles. Both developed in a part of the world where the climate during the winter can be very harsh. Good protection against the elements was essential to their survival, and this is what shaped the appearance of both breeds, along similar lines.

FELINE CHARACTERISTICS		NOTES
Starting out	A breed that has been shaped by the landscape in which it evolved.	
Personality	Friendly, with an unusual triple purring ability.	Gets along with dogs.
Appearance	Varies, with these cats looking larger in the winter, because of their longer coats.	
At home	Recent studies have focused on the possible hypoallergenic nature of their coat. Findings suggest the breed may evoke a less strong allergic response in people sensitive to cats.	
Behavior	Active and jumps very well. Also males mature early, often at just five months old.	
Grooming	Not especially demanding, as the coat tends not to mat. Develop a routine.	
Common health issues	Golden Siberians may be affected by hypertrophic cardiomyopathy. Not common in other varieties.	Most common form of heart disease in cats. Causes thickening of the muscle, causing heart failure.

Low ears
It has relatively small, low ears with furnishings and tufts of hair to protect against the cold.

Patterning
Tabby markings are common, with a white blaze between the eyes, extending down onto to the chest.

Lifestyle

In spite of their size, Siberians are surprisingly agile cats. They may leap up onto a shelf and wander along it, without knocking off any items. Although they settle well and build up a strong bond with other family members, they do retain an independent streak and like to explore outdoors, being undeterred by bad weather. The coat is much more profuse in the winter, becoming lighter during the summer. More grooming is necessary during the spring, when the winter coat is being shed.

Tufted paws
It has large paws, often with tufts of fur.

10. Longcoated Persian Cross

There are sometimes unplanned matings that occur between purebred and nonpedigree cats, resulting in kittens that are likely to show the characteristics of both parents. There is, however, no way of being able to predict the precise appearance of the young.

History

Encounters of this type are always likely to result in kittens, because of the peculiar reproductive biology of cats. Female cats, called queens, do not ovulate on a regular basis as part of a reproductive cycle. Instead, they release ova (eggs) as a result of mating, which serves significantly to increase the chances of successful fertilization. This is why in a town particularly, unneutered female cats will very soon end up being pregnant, as they are living at much greater densities than would be the case in the wild, where a single pair of wild cats may occupy an area of 3–4 sq. miles (7.8–10.3 sq. km). It is also important to remember that a female may mate several times in succession with a number of males, which means that a single litter can consist of kittens that have different fathers.

Impacts

A number of attractive crosses have resulted from such matings, and deliberate pairings between nonpedigree and purebred cats have then helped in various cases to develop breeds such as the Selkirk Rex (see page 75). It is much simpler to continue crossing with purebred stock that already has a stable genetic base, in terms of appearance, when seeking to develop a recognizable type. This approach also allows new colors or patterns to be introduced easily.

FELINE CHARACTERISTICS

For Feline Characteristics, see page 73

Head
The shape of the head is more angular than that of a true Persian, although littermates from such pairings can vary widely in appearance.

Coat
The coat is much less profuse than in the case of a Persian.

Feet
The legs are longer, although the paws are still large.

Cat types for people who may not have a lot of space in their homes, perhaps have young children who may struggle to handle a larger cat safely, or simply believe that small is beautiful.

Longhaired Munchkin

Siamese

Singapura

Small Cats

This group has grown significantly over recent years. This is probably a reflection of the fact that living spaces today are smaller, and more cats are being treated as house cats, kept indoors away from the dangers of traffic. There is also a fashion, inspired in part by celebrities, toward keeping smaller cats and dogs, humanizing them, and treating them more as little people than pets.

Another significant factor has been the development of the Munchkin breed (see page 82 and page 85), which has facilitated the creation of many miniaturized forms of existing breeds, as a result of its distinctive short-legged appearance. Although the origins of many of these cats can be traced back to natural mutations in street cats, the irony is that members of this group now rank among the most expensive of purebreds.

Small cats will generally settle well in the home, but it is important to bear in mind that all the short-legged varieties are unable to jump as effectively as breeds with longer legs. This, in turn, means that they can be much more vulnerable outside, if faced with potential predators or simply an aggressive dog. It is therefore important to try to contain them in a safe area if they are wandering outside. It may be necessary to set up an outdoor cattery, in the form of a well-insulated shed with a wire mesh run attached for this purpose, with a connecting door on the floor of the run.

Shorthaired Munchkin

Bambino Dwarf

1. Bambino Dwarf

This is a breed that most people either love or hate. There is little room for indifference in this case. Although the Bambino Dwarf is not yet firmly established, it has started to gain show recognition and is building up an international following.

History

This breed was created in 2005 by Pat and Stephanie Osborne of the HolyMoly Cattery, based in Arkansas. The description of "bambino" was inspired by Pat's Italian background and can be translated as "little one." This not only refers to the size of these cats, but also to the fact that they are playful throughout their lives. The Bambino is a hairless, short-legged cat, which has resulted from combining the key features of the Sphynx (see page 149) and Munchkin (see page 82), respectively. A separate bloodline, based on Munchkins imported from the U.S. is being developed in England. Other catteries with these cats exist in Spain and the Netherlands. Some believe these cats may be more suitable for allergy sufferers, but this is not definitely proven as yet.

Appearance

The almost total absence of hair means that these small cats reveal the color of their underlying skin. This can vary from pink to blackish tones, depending on the individual's markings. They all generally display some evident traces of a coat on the extremities of the body. Their most striking feature is often their eyes, which can vary quite widely in color. Some Bambinos have green eyes for example, and others may have blue eyes or odd eyes.

FELINE CHARACTERISTICS		NOTES
Starting out	A breed for indoors, rather than a neighborhood cat.	Not widely available at present.
Personality	Affectionate and playful by nature.	
Appearance	Unmistakable, due to its short legs and lack of fur.	Variable, individual patterning on the skin.
At home	Ideal companion breed but better kept as a pet on its own, rather than with a dog.	Rough and tumble games not to be encouraged.
Behavior	Curious and inquisitive, with a desire to explore its surroundings.	
Grooming	Lack of fur does not mean no grooming is required. Wiping of the skin needed.	
Common health issues	Vulnerable to sunburn if allowed outdoors and is at risk of skin injuries.	

Prominent ears
Tall, prominent ears give these cats a very alert appearance.

Wrinkly skin
Pale-colored Bambinos are especially vulnerable to sunburn and should be kept indoors. The wrinkling is a feature of the breed.

Tapered tail
The tail is long, relatively narrow, and tapers along its length.

2. Kinkalow

This breed is another short-legged creation, developed in part from Munchkin stock, and is currently rare but growing in numbers and popularity. It is now being exhibited, with the result that more breeders are becoming aware of its existence.

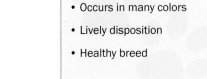
History

The Kinkalow was developed by an American breeder named Terri Harris, who crossed American Curls (see page 145), with their distinctive ears, to Munchkins, which are characterized by their short legs and friendly nature. Both the Kinkalow's ancestral breeds originated from spontaneous mutations that occurred in domestic street cats. Perhaps unsurprisingly therefore, Kinkalows themselves are very well adjusted, with easygoing, affable temperaments. They can potentially be bred in a very wide range of colors and patterns, although this aspect of breeding has yet to be explored in detail. They are quite healthy individuals, in spite of their short legs and relatively long bodies, plus their curled ears, but they are likely to come off worse in any fight with ordinary neighborhood cats, and so it is safer to keep them indoors.

Key features

Just as in the case of the American Curl, Kinkalows can be bred in any color, with the key feature being their ear shape. At birth, all the kittens in the litter will have what appear to be normal ears, but a percentage of these will soon start to curl, within ten days, enabling them to be distinguished easily. This particular feature is now more prominent in American Curl stock than in the past and is very evident in Kinkalows.

FELINE CHARACTERISTICS		NOTES
Starting out	Curled ears mean these cats are less suitable for homes with younger children.	Another rare breed at the moment.
Personality	Friendly and well-adjusted cats, as reflected by their ancestry.	Developed from mutations that occurred in ordinary domestic cats.
Appearance	Short-legged, with their curled ears giving an alert appearance.	Many Kinkalows display individual patterning.
At home	Thrives indoors but may be vulnerable to dogs and other cats outdoors.	
Behavior	Eager to investigate, as well as attentive. A keen watcher of what is going on.	
Grooming	No different from that of an ordinary domestic cat.	Those with long coats will need more grooming than shorthairs.
Common health issues	No significant health problems recorded but check that the ears are clean.	

Curled-up ears
The ears are curled up at the tips and directed inward.

Gender coloration
Calico (tortoiseshell-and-white) coloring indicates a female.

Long tail
It is a relatively long tail, quite broad at the base.

3. Longhaired Munchkin

The controversy surrounding this breed has died down as it has become better known, and people have been able to see that such cats are healthy and can live as long as other cats, in addition to being very friendly.

AT A GLANCE
- Unmistakable appearance
- Minimal grooming needs
- Able to run well
- Affectionate nature

History

The origins of the Munchkin date back to 1983, when a pregnant stray cat being chased by a dog was rescued from under a truck and adopted by music teacher Sandra Hochenedel in Louisiana. This cat, christened Blackberry, then gave birth to some short-legged kittens. But it was not until 1991 that the breed became widely known, thanks to a television broadcast organized by The International Cat Association (TICA) from Madison Square Garden. Twelve years later, TICA then granted the breed Championship status—equivalent to full show recognition. In the case of longhaired Munchkins, the coat is silky and semi-long, and this simplifies the grooming process compared with many other recognized longhaired breeds.

Unsubstantiated fears

There was real concern at the outset that the Munchkin might suffer from intervertebral disk and other spinal problems, as seen in Dachshunds and some other dogs, because of their long bodies and short legs. Detailed studies followed and gave the Munchkin a clean bill of health, but in spite of this, and its growing popularity, the breed has yet to obtain universal acceptance. Devotees now exist in many countries, however, ranging from England to South Africa and Australia.

FELINE CHARACTERISTICS		NOTES
Starting out	A distinctive cat that should prove to be a great companion.	
Personality	Friendly, well-balanced temperament.	Reflects its origins, being bred from an ordinary street cat.
Appearance	Short-legged, with an otherwise typical domestic cat appearance.	
At home	Affectionate and has a well-adjusted nature.	
Behavior	Very agile and can run fast without difficulty if required.	Not able to jump well on its short legs.
Grooming	Needs no more care than an ordinary domestic cat.	Longhaired Munchkins need more grooming than those with short coats.
Common health issues	Contrary to initial fears, there are no specific health problems in this breed.	

Upright tail
This is carried upright when the cat is moving.

White blaze
A white blaze is present between the eyes of this calico individual, which is a female, thanks to its tortoiseshell patterning.

Feet
These should be round in shape and compact and should point forward.

4. MiniPer

This scaled-down form of the Persian (see page 73) is significantly smaller in size, but otherwise basically identical in appearance and temperament. It is also important to remember that it will require the same amount of daily grooming as its larger relative.

History

While reducing the size of breeds to create new ones is well established in dog breeding circles, this is the first example that has occurred in cats. Miniaturization has been achieved by selecting the smallest cats and pairing these together. It is controversial, too, because of fears over inbreeding, and the fact that in dogs, smaller examples of a breed tend to be less sound than their original, bigger form. Already within the field of the MiniPer, three different sizes are often distinguished, on the basis of the weight of the adult cats. The largest of these is the MiniPer Toy, averaging 6.5–7 lbs. (2.9–3.1 kg), with the MiniPer Teacup varying between 4.5–6 lbs. (2–2.7 kg). The smallest members of this group, and the most expensive, are described as MiniPer Micros. They are just 3–4 lbs. (1.4–1.8 kg) when adult, whereas a typical standard Persian may weigh 10–12 lbs. (4.5–5.4 kg).

Scaling down

MiniPer kittens are tiny at birth, with Micros being roughly the length of a woman's index finger. All parts of their bodies reflect their scaled-down proportions, being consistent in size, and potentially, they can be created in a similarly wide range of colors. They also need careful daily grooming, in order to prevent their coats from becoming matted and to protect them against fur balls when they are shedding. Some breeders, however, do not distinguish between the longcoated "true" Persian form of these dwarf cats and a shorter-haired type, which is modeled on the Exotic.

FELINE CHARACTERISTICS		NOTES
Starting out	Uncommon and expensive. A dwarf form of a standard Persian.	The smallest examples are often described as Tea Cup kittens.
Personality	Relaxed, gentle, and friendly, making an ideal companion.	
Appearance	A scaled-down version of a Persian, with a flattened face.	Can be hard to tell the likely adult size of kittens.
At home	Peaceful, but small size and placid nature means these cats are best kept indoors.	
Behavior	Settles well but obviously its surroundings need to reflect its smaller size.	
Grooming	Will be required on a daily basis, with combing and brushing necessary.	
Common health issues	Similar to those recorded in its Persian ancestor. Tear staining most evident.	Dwarfism itself does not appear to have affected the health of these cats.

Face shape
MiniPers—whatever their size—still retain the same flattened facial profile as standard Persians, and this can lead to tear staining on the fur at the corner of the eyes nearest to the nose.

Coat length
Whereas standard Persians are recognized as a distinctive breed from the shorter-coated Exotic, this distinction does not apply in MiniPers. This cat has a full-length coat.

Leg length
Their legs are in proportion to the rest of their bodies, in keeping with their miniaturized appearance.

5. Elf Cat

The Elf Cat, originating in the U.S., is one of the most recent additions to the list of new breeds that are currently being created. It represents a combination of the relatively hairless Sphynx (see page 149) breed crossed with the American Curl (see page 105).

(see page 149)
(see page 105)

AT A GLANCE
- Highly individual
- An indoor cat
- Needs regular washing
- Can look worried!

History

Two long-standing breeders of Sphynx cats, Karen Nelson and Kristen Leedom, decided to develop a separate lineage by introducing the curled ears of the American Curl into the Sphynx bloodline. A sound genetic base for the Elf Cat has been created by enlisting the help of other breeders widely distributed across the U.S., including those in California, Idaho, Michigan, Illinois, Arizona, and Georgia. The use of ordinary Domestic Shorthairs has also helped in this regard, by introducing a variety of new genes into the bloodlines, and so preventing inbreeding, which often occurs in the early stages when a new breed is being developed. In fact, the breed was not created until 2007, after careful consideration of the breeding plan, which was drawn up with the aid of feline geneticists.

Elf care

Taking care of these cats is quite straightforward, but the relative absence of a coat does not mean that they require no grooming. In fact, a gentle rubdown every week is to be recommended, partly to keep the coat free from grease. The ears, too, should be regularly and carefully cleaned, without poking down inside the ear canal itself. The actual curl of the ears varies between individuals, but it should lie somewhere between 90 and 180 degrees. Elf Cats have proved to be friendly by nature, with gentle, intelligent dispositions.

FELINE CHARACTERISTICS		NOTES
Starting out	Uncommon at present, but growing in numbers. Best suited to being a house cat.	Occurs potentially in a very wide range of colors.
Personality	An ideal companion, being very affectionate and can be devoted to its owner.	
Appearance	Fine covering of fur, curled ears, and wrinkles, which can create a worried frown.	Feels warm to the touch, in common with similar hairless breeds.
At home	Agile nature means these cats can climb or jump up onto furniture easily.	
Behavior	Quite extrovert and very playful and intelligent by nature.	
Grooming	Wipe these cats over each week using a damp chamois leather.	Do not forget to clean the ears carefully.
Common health issues	None, but obviously more susceptible to injuries in fights if allowed outdoors.	Best kept as an indoor pet, away from climatic extremes.

Large ears
These are curled over at their tips and extend outward from the sides of the head, emphasizing its width.

Some fur present
It is a very fine, downy covering of fur on the body. Coloration varies widely. Black cats, for example, will appear completely different, with their entire bodies being dark.

Long tail
This is a feature inherited from the Sphynx, tapering toward the tip.

Wrinkled skin
This is a feature of the Elf Cat, with the wrinkling becoming less pronounced when the cat is standing up, although it tends to be more consistent on the forehead.

6. Shortcoated Munchkin

The Munchkin exists in a shorthaired form, too. It has had a dramatic impact on cat breeding in recent years, paving the way for many new, short-legged breeds to be developed, but it also remains popular in its own right.

History

The breed's name originated from that given to the little people in the musical *The Wizard of Oz*. There are no restrictions relating to either coloration or patterning in the case of these cats. The fur of the shorthaired version of the breed is relatively short with a plush texture and surprisingly weather resistant. An unusual aspect in the development of both the longhaired and shorthaired forms of this breed is the fact that any outcrosses had to be nonpedigrees cats. As a result, self (solid) colors, such as the black seen here, may tend to be seen less often, when compared with tabby forms.

Breeding

There were persistent reports of similar, short-legged cats well before this breed came into existence, dating back in the U.S. to 1944, and another possible strain was lost in Europe around this stage because of the Second World War. It was almost immediately apparent that the short-legged appearance of the Munchkin was due to an autosomal recessive mutation. This means that when a Munchkin is paired to another member of the breed, they will produce kittens that are all Munchkins, but none results in the first generation, when a Munchkin is paired with a normal street cat. If you want a breed that cannot steal food off work surfaces by jumping up, then a Munchkin is a good choice. You may not find it straightforward to catch one of these cats, though, as they can run fast.

FELINE CHARACTERISTICS

For Feline Characteristics, see page 82

Sloping back
The back slopes slightly upward, from the head to the tail.

High cheekbones
The head is wedge-shaped, with the cheekbones set high. The eyes are walnut-shaped.

Short legs
The front legs are straight, although they might sometimes be slightly bowed and can be slightly shorter than the hind legs.

7. Siamese

Siamese cats are one of the most distinctive and well-known breeds. They are characterized by their sleek, short coats and pointed markings, which refer to the darker areas of fur present on the extremities of their bodies.

History

The appearance of these cats has changed significantly, however, as the result of breeding in the West. They were first imported from Thailand in the second half of the last century, at a stage when their heads were much more rounded than they are today. This older type of Siamese is now being recreated in the West (see page 39) as a distinct breed that stands apart from the triangular face and very angular lines that characterize modern show bloodlines. Another change, which has not been universally accepted, has been the increasing number of Siamese colors recognized by some show-promoting organizations. Nontraditional forms such as the red point remain controversial with some breeders.

Temperament

Siamese are a sexually precocious breed, so be prepared to have a young queen neutered at an early stage, possibly at three to four months old. This operation, called spaying, will avoid the risk of an unwanted litter. This is also important for domestic peace, too, as these cats will call very loudly and persistently when seeking a mate, keeping both your family and even near neighbors awake. Siamese are normally spayed via an incision made in the midline on the underside of the body, rather than on the flank. It will prevent their fur color from darkening conspicuously on the side of the body. This otherwise happens because the body area is temporarily cooler here as the fur grows back, after being shaved for surgery.

FELINE CHARACTERISTICS		NOTES
Starting out	The coloration on the points develops as the kitten grows older.	Siamese are born white.
Personality	Dominant but affectionate, demanding attention. Not a very tranquil companion.	
Appearance	Color changes with ages, with shading on the flanks becoming prominent.	This is particularly evident in dark varieties such as the sealpoint.
At home	Athletic, likes to climb both indoors and out. A climbing frame recommended.	
Behavior	Sexually precious, with queens being particularly vocal when calling.	
Grooming	Straightforward, requiring little more than stroking.	
Common health issues	Squinting and kinked tails largely bred out of modern bloodlines. At risk from respiratory infections.	Especially likely to suffer from diarrhea caused by intolerance to cow's milk.

Blue eyes
The vivid blue coloration is seen in all varieties, irrespective of the point coloration.

Balance aid
Long and narrow, the tail helps the cat balance.

Markings
The body extremities— the points—are darker in color than the body.

8. Napoleon

One of the very latest breeds to be created, the Napoleon has arisen from deliberate crossbreeding between the Munchkin, accounting for its very short stature, and Persian Longhairs. The latter's influence is apparent not just in its coat length but also its temperament.

History

The emergence of the short-legged Munchkin has transformed the breeding of purebred cats, in North America especially where this breed originated. The development of the Napoleon itself began in 1995, when a breeder of Basset Hounds—dogs characterized by their short legs —was inspired to start a breeding program. He chose the name of Napoleon to reflect the short stature of these cats, as this was a noted characteristic of the famous French ruler Napoleon Bonaparte. In terms of temperament, these cats display the friendly nature of both the parent breeds, being relaxed and delighting in human company.

Appearance

It is important to remember that the Napoleon is a relative newcomer on the feline scene, and so individuals are likely to display more variance in appearance than in the case of cats belonging to more established breeds. Napoleon breeders are seeking to retain the rounded face of the Persian but not to encourage the extreme snub nose associated with this breed. Equally, they are not seeking to develop the very long coat that typifies the Persian Longhair.

Ears
These are relatively large, compared with those of Persian Longhairs.

Color
Napoleons are being bred in a wide range of colors and pattern forms.

Legs
These are short and round, reflecting the stance of their Munchkin ancestor.

FELINE CHARACTERISTICS		NOTES
Starting out	Another of the recent crosses involving the short-legged Munchkin breed.	It has been crossbred with the Persian to create this new breed.
Personality	More active than a Persian, but still possesses a gentle, home-loving nature.	
Appearance	Facial appearance likened to that of a baby doll, with appealing round eyes.	Retains the short legs of the Munchkin.
At home	An attractive, friendly nature has helped ensure growing popularity.	
Behavior	Likes human company but tends to be more playful than a true Persian.	
Grooming	Regular combing and brushing required, to prevent any matting.	The fur is not as profuse as in the case of a Persian.
Common health issues	None recorded. Might inherit kidney problems from Persian ancestry.	Facial shape less extreme, so tear staining not really a problem.

9. Singapura

For a number of years after its discovery on the streets of Singapore, the Singapura was accepted as being the smallest breed in the world. As with other Oriental breeds, their grooming needs are minimal, as they lack a dense undercoat.

History

The breed's origins have been challenged over recent years, because of supposed discrepancies with the paperwork surrounding the original importation into the U.S. and recent DNA analysis that suggests a close relationship with the Burmese. The accepted version of events, however, is that a cat-loving couple named Hal and Tommy Meadows discovered the feral ancestors of the breed living on the streets of Singapore. They brought back four of these cats when they returned to the U.S. in 1975. These formed the foundation stock for today's bloodline, with another breeder discovering a virtually identical cat six years later in a cat rescue center in Singapore. This was also imported to the U.S., and played its part in the breed's development.

Coloration
The breed's coloration is described as sepia agouti, with brown ticking offset against a ground color described as "warm old ivory."

Small body
The narrow body shape and small size of these cats helps reinforce their alternative name of "drain cat," reflecting their origins.

Ticked tabby
As a ticked tabby, the Singapura has dark tips to its individual hairs and banding down their length.

Relationships

The Singapura is recognized as being a natural breed. DNA studies have confirmed that its genetic base is very small, as might be anticipated from its origins, and in spite of extensive searching in Singapore, no cats showing similar markings have been seen since the last individual around 30 years ago. This may be, however, because the area where the Singapura originated has been subjected to extensive redevelopment, and the feral cat population there would undoubtedly have been displaced. Spotting such cats was not easy, though, as they were often shy and hid out of sight in storm drains. Even today, Singapuras are still described as "drain cats" for this reason.

FELINE CHARACTERISTICS		NOTES
Starting out	Another striking breed resulting from a natural mutation.	A ticked tabby, only available in one color.
Personality	Curious and lively, integrating well with its owners.	
Appearance	Surprisingly small, with very cuddly appearance.	Singapuras have tended to increase slightly in size since they became known in the West.
At home	Quite affectionate and home-loving. Likes to curl up in small spaces.	
Behavior	Likes to climb and may seek a high vantage point in a room.	
Grooming	Very straightforward, as it does not have much undercoat.	
Common health issues	None, although occasionally, queens may suffer from uterine inertia.	Caused by weak muscles, so young must be born by Cesarean section.

10. Sokoke

These blotched tabbies have both an unusual marbled appearance and breed history, being one of the few contemporary cat breeds to come out of Africa. Their behavior is unusual, too—for example, with the male cat assisting his partner to rear their kittens.

AT A GLANCE

- Unique pattern
- African origins
- Gentle nature
- May live in family groups

FELINE CHARACTERISTICS		NOTES
Starting out	A localized, naturally occurring form of tabby that emerged in Kenya.	One of the very few breeds of domestic cat to come out of Africa.
Personality	Friendly, well-adjusted nature, proving affectionate to family members.	
Appearance	Distinctive tabby, with markings resembling wood grain on the flanks.	Agouti ticking may extend right down the tail in some cases.
At home	Settles well in the home and prefers relatively warm surroundings.	
Behavior	Male cats help look after the kittens in this case. Weaning can be slow.	
Grooming	Combing and brushing required, as will keep these cats looking immaculate.	Relative absence of an undercoat simplifies the grooming process.
Common health issues	Sensitive to cold and can be vulnerable to various infections.	Be sure to keep its vaccinations up to date, as in other cases.

Variable eye coloration
This can range from amber to a light shade of green.

Well-defined whisker pads
The nose is broad, while the head overall is small in relation to the body.

Classic coloration
The brown (black) classic tabby form is the accepted variety, but lynx (tabby) points do occur occasionally.

History

A localized population of these cats had been living in the Arabuko-Sokoke forest on the coast of Kenya, possibly for centuries before they were discovered by two European women in 1978. Their native name is Khadzonzos, which was given to the breed by the Giriama tribe, and translates literally as appearing "like tree bark," describing their very distinctive patterning. Further investigation into the origins of these cats using DNA analysis suggests they belong to the Asian group, being descended from the Arabian form of the African Wild Cat (*Felis silvestris lybica*). Originating from a warm area of the world, they lack a significant undercoat, so their fur lies close against the body, reinforcing the impact of their patterning.

Breed development

Two of these cats were imported to Denmark and exhibited for the first time at a show held in Copenhagen in 1984. Three more followed in 1991, and then after the turn of the century, a number of so-called New Line Sokokes were imported to broaden the gene pool, both to Europe itself and to the U.S. Sokokes have proved to dislike cold weather and also to be susceptible to relatively minor infections to which European cats have resistance, and so it is critical that they are fully vaccinated, and also, they should not be encouraged to wander, where they could come into contact with other cats. They actually have a distinctive way of walking, almost on tiptoe.

Korat

Cat types for people who appreciate beauty and elegance in the world around them, as well as style and personality, too.

Somali

Gorgeous Cats

It is not just coloration that can be significant as far as cats are concerned, when it comes to determining their attractiveness. Their shape, form, and patterning can all be important. The eyes of various breeds are often an especially overlooked aspect of their appeal. The size and shape of the eyes, not to mention their coloration, can significantly enhance a breed's beauty, as has been recognized for centuries.

In the *Cat Book Poems*, which were produced during the Ayudhya period of Siamese history (1350–1767) in the vicinity of present-day Thailand, the color of the Korat's eyes was described as corresponding to that of lotus leaves. They contrasted with the silvery coloration of its fur, which was popularly believed to signify wealth.

Since then, there have been many other breeds of cats developed primarily just to look gorgeous, with this trend continuing even today, although it has to be said that true beauty in the case of cats is in the eyes of the beholder! This will hopefully be a long-standing association between you, and having compatible personalities will be vital, as in any successful relationship.

Russian

1. Australian Mist

Formerly called the Spotted Mist, these attractive cats have wonderfully expressive large eyes. Even better, though, their docile nature means that they make wonderful companions for young and old alike. Remarkably, however, these cats are still not really known outside Australia.

History

Abyssinian and Burmese cats were selected by Dr. Truda Straede, the founder of this breed, to contribute to its ancestry, along with ordinary nonpedigree cats. Her original aim was to create a breed with a spotted coat, but subsequently, cats showing a marbled pattern rather than spotting in their coats were also recognized. This necessitated a change in the breed's name to that used today. Each of these patterns can be developed in association with any one of the seven colors associated with this emerging breed. There are brown, blue, chocolate, lilac, caramel, gold, or peach varieties. The coat itself is soft and glossy without a dense undercoat, giving these cats a sleek appearance.

Relatively large body
Well muscled and strong, with a broad chest.

Broad head
Slightly rounded, with the ears quite widely spaced. The eyes are large and round.

FELINE CHARACTERISTICS		NOTES
Starting out	An uncommon breed outside Australia.	Used to be called the Spotted Mist.
Personality	Gentle-natured, quite relaxed, and friendly.	
Appearance	Medium-size, with attractive patterning reinforced by the short coat.	The shape of the head emphasizes the breed's expressive eyes.
At home	Kittens are very playful but do not display a strong instinct to hunt.	
Behavior	Will seek out human company, but gets along well with other cats and dogs.	Not inclined to scratch, so a good choice for a home with children.
Grooming	Very straightforward, with stroking helping to improve the gloss on the coat.	
Common health issues	None generally recognized, but as with all cats, keep vaccinations current.	

Misty appearance

Unlike other breeds, the gorgeous appearance of the Australian Mist stems from three rather than two different elements in its coat. There is the pale background color, on top of which the spotted patterning is superimposed. There is also ticking evident in areas where there is no spotting. This creates the characteristic misty effect. Another feature making the Australian Mist almost unique in the cat world is the fact that its ancestry can be traced right back to the start, through breeding records.

Short coat
Glossy coat, emphasizing the random, spotted patterning. The spots vary in size and shape.

2. Balinese

These cats have no direct link to the Indonesian island of Bali, but breeders decided that their graceful elegance and movement resembled that of native dancers on the island, so they became known as Balinese. They are closely related to Siamese (see page 86).

(see page 86)

AT A GLANCE

- Beautiful appearance
- Semi-longhair
- Graceful movement
- Range of varieties

FELINE CHARACTERISTICS		NOTES
Starting out	A Western creation, in spite of its Asian name, being a longhaired Siamese.	
Personality	Lively and demonstrative, actively seeking out human company.	
Appearance	Pointed coloration, with the extremities of the body differing in color.	Occurs in all Siamese colors. Distinctive blue eyes.
At home	Can be surprisingly vocal, with kittens sometimes rather wild at times.	
Behavior	Rated as one of the most intelligent of all cat breeds. Has a very playful nature.	Sexually precocious, so early neutering is advisable.
Grooming	Straightforward in spite of the long coat, because of the lack of undercoat.	The tail displays a very distinctive plume, but the coat is flat.
Common health issues	Can be vulnerable to upper respiratory infections.	

History

It is unclear as to when or how the recessive longhaired gene entered Siamese bloodlines, but this had certainly occurred by the late 1920s, if not earlier. Odd individuals of this type born to Siamese mothers had longer coats than normal and a well-plumed tail. In the U.S., enthusiasts decided to develop these longhaired cats into a distinctive breed. These longhaired Siamese were then finally recognized under the name of Balinese in 1961. There is a difference in the type of Balinese, just as there is with Siamese, with the traditional form of the Balinese having a more rounded, less angular face. It has proved to be a very intelligent, affectionate breed, as an additional bonus to its good looks.

Colors

Balinese were originally bred in the four traditional Siamese variants—seal point, blue point, lilac point, and chocolate point—but just as occurred in Siamese, the range of available colors has increased significantly over recent years. There is still controversy over their recognition, though, so new colors such as red point and tortie point are sometimes grouped together under the breed name of Javanese, which maintains the Asian theme, with Java lying close to Bali. One difference compared with Siamese, however, is that these cats have quieter voices.

Large, pricked ears
These have wide bases and have longer hair inside, described as furnishings.

Pale body
This is always lighter in color than the points, but shading may develop in older cats.

Long tail
Relatively slender tail, with a good covering of hair.

3. Bombay

Another Burmese (see page 56) derivative, with a wonderfully lustrous black coat contrasting with the breed's eyes, which tend to be coppery, but can be green. The breed was named after the Indian city of Bombay, which is better known as Mumbai today.

AT A GLANCE
- A mini panther
- Easy-care coat
- Not a fussy feeder
- Happy in canine company

History

There are now two distinct varieties of Bombay cats, with the original American strain having been developed during 1958 in Kentucky by a breeder named Nikki Horner, who was seeking to create a strain of miniature black panthers. She relied on crosses between American Shorthairs (see page 104) and Burmese for this purpose. British breeders, however, followed a different route, using their native shorthaired breed, with the same aim. In both cases, occasional sable-colored kittens crop up in Bombay litters, as a reminder of the Burmese contribution to the development of these breeds. The coat texture is very distinctive, being short, with a texture like satin. It is very glossy and sleek, outlining the cat's body, and consistently colored to the roots.

Care matters

Bombay cats generally have very healthy appetites, and so they can become overweight quite easily. This will then spoil their svelte outline, aside from potentially causing health problems. The distinctive coat needs very little grooming, and regular stroking is frequently enough to keep it looking at its best. It remains consistent in length and appearance throughout the year. In terms of temperament, the Bombay is usually well disposed to dogs but may not get along so well with other cats.

FELINE CHARACTERISTICS		NOTES
Starting out	Highly distinctive breed, due to its appearance. Quiet by nature.	
Personality	Can be rather nervous but affectionate and friendly to family members.	
Appearance	Stunning black coloration and copper-colored eyes, with a very glossy coat.	
At home	Prefers quiet, tranquil surroundings, with a set routine.	Probably not the best choice for a home with noisy teenagers.
Behavior	Can be distressed by loud noises and can be rather nervous outdoors.	Keep these cats in, especially at night when fireworks may be let off.
Grooming	Very straightforward. Stroking will help maintain the sheen and remove loose hairs.	
Common health issues	Can be vulnerable to protrusion of the third eyelid, called cherry eye.	Bombay kittens are occasionally born with a cleft palate.

Rounded head
The muzzle is short and there is a moderate "stop"—change in profile—between the eyes.

Rounded feet
The legs themselves are in proportion to the body, with the chest rounded, too.

Medium-size body
It can take as long as two years for the full beauty of the Bombay's coat to become totally apparent.

4. Egyptian Mau

One of the most striking of the tabby breeds, the Egyptian Mau is a beautiful cat, both in terms of its looks and its personality. The silver tabby form seen here is especially attractive, with its green eyes highlighted with black lids.

AT A GLANCE

- Striking patterning
- Individual markings
- Relatively small breed
- Short, silky coat

History

Although the Egyptian Mau's large eyes set against its relatively small head can convey what may sometimes resemble a worried appearance, these cats are quite placid and relaxed as companions. Originally descended from street cats living in Cairo, Egypt, the majority of this breed's development has occurred in the U.S., where it is now quite commonly seen at shows. Currently, however, it is virtually unknown in Europe, where breeders have concentrated instead on Oriental spotted tabbies. In terms of temperament, Egyptian Maus are friendly, confident cats that like to be involved in family life. They have an unusual range of vocalizations, including a rather distinctive chortle that is often heard when interacting with their owners. The breed displays a natural athleticism, too, with few cats being faster when running.

Unique patterning

It is said that the Egyptian Mau is the only domestic cat that is naturally spotted in appearance. The spots themselves are randomly distributed over the entire body and are very variable in size as well as shape. Only down the back do they run in organized parallel lines, sometimes fusing into a stripe at the base of the tail. The most important aspect of the patterning is that it needs to stand out very clearly.

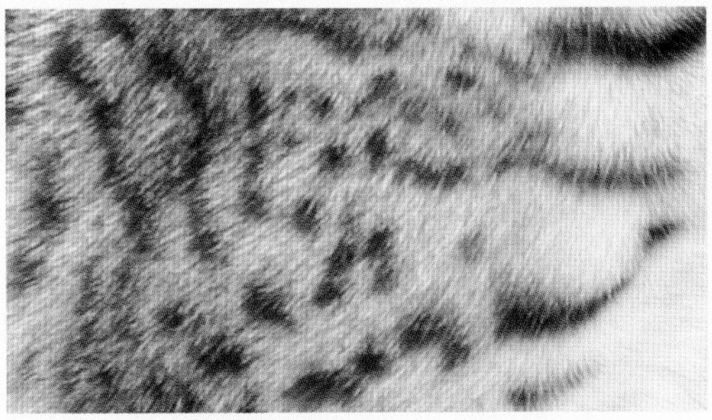

FELINE CHARACTERISTICS

For Feline Characteristics, see page 61

Eye lines
These are especially prominent, called mascara lines because of their dark appearance.

Small paws
The paws have dark undersides and relatively long toes. Random tabby barring is evident on the legs.

Tapering tail
Of moderate length, and displays tabby barring, ending in a dark tip.

5. European Burmese

The cuddly and colorful appearance of these cats, resulting from their soft, dense coat, is reinforced by their affectionate, companionable nature. Although closely related to Siamese (see page 86), they also have a more laid-back temperament, in terms of their personality.

(see page 86)

History

The foundation stock for these Burmese is no different than that responsible for American lines of Burmese. The original forerunners of these cats were exported to Europe from America, but once there, these cats were evolved on different lines, which explains the variation that exists in their appearance today. Part of this is a reflection of the range of recognized Siamese varieties in Europe, where the red gene is accepted, although it is not a traditional Siamese color. The introduction of this characteristic to European Burmese bloodlines has, in turn, increased the number of colors to ten, including colors such as cream (seen here) and red, not to mention tortoiseshell varieties, which are not recognized in the case of American Burmese.

Looks and personality

It is not just coloration that varies, but there are physical distinctions, too, to the extent that these cats are exhibited in separate classes, as a result of their differences in appearance. The greater input of the Siamese into European bloodlines means that their eyes are curved downward. In contrast, those of American Burmese are much more rounded. The temperament of both breeds is similar, though, and their amiable natures mean they are generally happy sharing the home with a dog or even other cats.

Large eyes
These are well-spaced, with a curved top line and a more rounded lower line.

FELINE CHARACTERISTICS		NOTES
Starting out	Less of an extrovert than the closely related Siamese. Has a chunkier build.	
Personality	Friendly, affectionate, and not especially noisy nor frenetic by nature.	
Appearance	More angular head shape distinguishes this breed from its American relative.	
At home	Settles well and playful by nature. Needs plenty of attention.	Can suffer hair loss through excessive grooming, which needs veterinary care.
Behavior	Likes to climb and play, and should be provided with suitable indoor facilities.	
Grooming	Coat care is straightforward, due to the lack of undercoat.	Brushing with a chamois leather imparts a good gloss to the coat.
Common health issues	So-called "cherry eye" does crop up, with red areas at the corner of the eyes. This needs surgical correction.	Not affected by the head or heart defects that can arise in U.S. Burmese.

Medium-length tail
This tapers a little along its length, ending in a rounded tip.

Small feet
Oval in shape, with the legs themselves relatively slender.

6. Korat

This ancient Thai breed perfectly reflects how a silvery-blue coat combined with a contrasting eye color can be a gorgeous combination. There is a lot of mythology attached to this breed in its homeland, and ownership is said to bring good fortune.

AT A GLANCE

- Unusual heart-shaped face
- Large, luminous eyes
- Unique coloration
- Slow to mature

History

The first examples of the breed reached the U.S. in 1959. The ancestry of today's cats traces back directly to those imported from Thailand. Unusually, no outcrossing to other breeds—so as to widen the color range, for example—has been permitted. This is a reflection of the very unique appearance of the Korat's coat. It is blue but has a very distinctive silvery tipping evident on the individual hairs. Their appearance is affected by the light, and this can result in what may appear to be a halo around the cat's body. The Korat's large eyes are also very distinctive, being a luminous shade of green.

Age considerations

This breed takes its English name from the province in northeastern Thailand where it was first bred perhaps more than 1,000 years ago. In its homeland, however, it is called Si-Sawat. This name describes its characteristic grayish-blue coloration, which corresponds to that of the seeds of the Sawat tree. Korats are relatively slow to mature, and it can take two years for kittens to develop their characteristic eye coloration. Up until this stage, their eyes are likely to be shades of yellow or amber.

FELINE CHARACTERISTICS		NOTES
Starting out	A beautiful and very distinctive breed, with a long history.	Lilac cats sometimes emerge in some lines of Korats.
Personality	A very determined breed, with a lively, playful, and companionable nature.	
Appearance	Defined by its color. Has a short, blue coat with silvery tipping and green eyes.	
At home	Can feel the cold because of the lack of insulation present in its coat.	Korats lack body fat under the skin, which would provide insulation.
Behavior	Displays a wide range of vocalizations and loves to play and climb.	
Grooming	Simply stroking the coat will usually suffice, helping maintain its condition.	Has a single coat, with no dense undercoat.
Common health issues	Susceptible to upper respiratory infections, like other Asian breeds.	Be sure to maintain protective vaccine cover throughout the cat's life.

Large ears
These have rounded tips and are located high on the head, contributing to the cat's alert expression.

Medium-length tail
This is thicker at the base and tapers along its length to a rounded tip.

Glossy coat
This forms a single layer, without a dense undercoat, so that the fur lies close to the body.

7. Russian

For many years, these cats were simply called Russian Blues, but thanks to the advent of white-and-black varieties that are now recognized for show purposes by some organizations, the description of "blue" has tended to be dropped from their name.

AT A GLANCE

• Very quiet cats

• Reputedly, a hypoallergenic breed

• Playful, loyal nature

• Reserved with strangers

FELINE CHARACTERISTICS		NOTES
Starting out	A natural, shorthaired breed, traditionally a silvery-blue color.	Formerly called the Russian Blue, but now other colors, including white, are bred.
Personality	Intelligent and playful, soon learning to bring a toy to its owner when wanting to play.	
Appearance	Medium-size, with a short, plush coat. Males tend to be slightly larger in size.	
At home	A particularly sensitive breed, which is shy and reserved with strangers.	Another breed from the far north said to be hypoallergenic.
Behavior	Tranquil nature and does not like a noisy environment. Likes to go outside.	
Grooming	Double coat is easy to keep in good condition by combing and brushing.	
Common health issues	DNA testing is eliminating the metabolic disease called gangliosidosis.	

History

This breed is closely linked with the port of Archangel, on Russia's north coast. It was from here that the breed was first taken to England in the 1860s by sailors, and it was then exhibited under the name of Archangel Cat. The future of the breed became uncertain at the end of the World War II, and crossings with Siamese were used, as a means of keeping it in existence. It was soon after this stage that Russians reached the U.S. Since then, careful selective breeding has removed most of the Siamese influence from Russian bloodlines, thereby recreating a breed whose actual origins have been lost in the mists of time.

Snake head
The head of the Russian is sometimes likened to that of a cobra, having both wedge-shaped and flat profiles.

Distinctive characteristics

The coat is silvery at its tips, creating a shimmering effect, with the eyes dark green in adult Russians, although as is usual in kittens, their eyes are blue at first. Pure coloration applies in the case of white and black variants of the breed. These are best known in Australia, where they were originally created in the 1970s. All Russians have a distinctive double coat, so-called because the undercoat is the same length as the top coat, creating a very dense yet soft fur, insulating them very effectively against the cold.

Coat
The breed is also well muscled, while retaining an elegance at the same time.

Dense coat
This feature causes the fur to stand away from the body rather than lying sleek.

8. Snowshoe

Although it may not look it, the Snowshoe has been a very controversial breed because of its origins. It also represents a particular challenge for exhibition breeders, because of the very precise nature of its markings, which cannot be predicted.

AT A GLANCE

- Very devoted companion
- Gets along well with children
- Has been known to swim
- Distinctive patterning

History

The origins of the Snowshoe date back to the 1960s. A Siamese cat kept by an American breeder named Dorothy Hinds-Dougherty, living in Philadelphia, gave birth to a litter of three kittens, all of whom displayed the characteristic white markings on their legs and feet. Eager to develop these features into a breed, their creator used bicolor American Shorthairs and Siamese for this purpose, but encountered considerable opposition from other Siamese breeders, who feared this distinctive white patching might become more prominent in their bloodlines. Ultimately, it fell to another breeder named Vikki Olander to obtain preliminary show recognition for the breed in 1974. These cats became known as Snowshoes because of their white feet.

Markings and behavior

A number of different genes are involved in the Snowshoe's appearance. The inverted V-shaped patterning on the face is not the result of the same genes that affect the patterning on the limbs, for example. Symmetry of markings is a vital feature of a good quality Snowshoe, but mismarked individuals can nevertheless make excellent pets. They are affectionate and intelligent, and often display an unusual affinity for water. Snowshoes can also be surprisingly vocal as well—a reflection of their Siamese ancestry.

Rounded head
This reflects the shorthair input into the breed's ancestry, being far less angular than in modern Siamese.

Blue eyes
These are a reflection of the Siamese's contribution to the breed's ancestry.

Coat color
Different colors are recognized by the various cat organizations in the case of this breed. The seal point seen here is universally recognized.

White at first
Kittens are born white, as in the case of Siamese, and start to gain their distinctive pointed patterning from one week old.

FELINE CHARACTERISTICS		NOTES
Starting out	Obtaining a perfectly marked individual is not straightforward.	Mismarked individuals have the same attributes, though, and will make good pets.
Personality	Friendly and affectionate nature but more placid than a Siamese.	
Appearance	Relatively large, recognized in a range of point colors, broken by white on the feet.	
At home	Does not like to be left for long periods on its own on a regular basis.	Think about obtaining a pair of kittens if you are out during the day.
Behavior	Will seek attention by meowing, but certainly not as noisy as Siamese.	Often displays a fascination with water.
Grooming	Relatively straightforward, with simple brushing and combing sufficing.	
Common health issues	Does not appear to suffer from any significant inherited disorders.	

9. Wild Abyssinian

These unusual cats are described as wild, in order to distinguish them from the ordinary Abyssinian (see page 44), which has been kept for more than a century. Both are ticked tabbies, with a striking coat pattern, and have proved to be intelligent, affectionate breeds.

(see page 44)

AT A GLANCE
- Unusual, rare breed
- Has ticked tabby patterning
- Friendly nature
- Playful disposition

FELINE CHARACTERISTICS		NOTES
Starting out	A rare breed, which appears to have become scarcer over recent years.	This is not a wild cat, nor related to the Abyssinian breed.
Personality	Relatively large and friendly cat with a playful side to its nature.	
Appearance	Bigger version of the Abyssinian, distinguished by the barring on its legs.	This is a ticked tabby, but its appearance is not as refined as in the Abyssinian.
At home	Typical well-balanced nature, reflecting its recent nonpedigree origins.	
Behavior	Independent, active side to its nature. Train this cat to come when called.	
Grooming	Straightforward, being a sleek shorthaired breed.	
Common health issues	None reported, but vaccinations are important in Asian breeds recently brought to the West.	

Other differences

The Wild Abyssinian is somewhat larger in size, compared with the Abyssinian, and has a very evident M-shaped "frown" marking on the head, which is a characteristic associated with tabbies in general and is a feature still seen in the Abyssinian. It is larger in size, too, and also has a more rounded, chunkier face. Since being discovered during the 1980s, and brought back to Massachusetts by Abyssinian enthusiast Tord Svenson, these cats have remained rare, in spite of their undeniable appeal.

History

The ancestors of the Wild Abyssinian were discovered living in a feral state in a rain forest in Singapore and have no link to Africa, where the Abyssinian itself originated. What is interesting, however, is the similarity in their markings. It is believed that the Wild Abyssinian of today is very similar to the original ancestors of the Abyssinian itself. It displays the typical alternating light and dark bands running down the individual hairs, yet it also shows tabby characteristics that have now been eliminated from the Abyssinian itself by selective breeding. These include the black circles of fur around the neck, known as necklaces, not to mention the tabby banding on the legs. The distribution of such patterning varies among individuals, enabling them to be told apart easily on this basis.

Tabby markings
These jet-black areas in the coat are a variable feature.

Tabby tail
The markings here are again variable but take the form of alternating light and dark rings.

Back of legs
Black fur present on the back of the hind legs, which is most apparent when the cat is standing or walking.

10. Somali

The dark area surrounding the eyes enhances the appeal of these cats, which represent the longhaired form of the Abyssinian. Not only are they graceful when moving, but the banding in their coat causes a shimmering effect when they are active.

AT A GLANCE

- Beautifully patterned coat
- Intelligent nature
- Long-lived
- Agile hunter

History

It took many years after the emergence of the first longhaired kitten in a litter of Abyssinians for cats of this type to be accepted for show purposes and developed into a separate breed. Today, however, having first gained acceptance in the U.S., the Somali has established a worldwide following. Its coat is not as profuse as that of some longhairs, such as the Persian, but there is still a noticeable ruff of long fur around the neck, which is particularly apparent over the winter months when the coat is at its most impressive. Somalis require more grooming at this stage, and especially in the spring, when this longer coat is being shed.

Grooming health

Like other longhairs, Somalis can be vulnerable to fur balls if they are not groomed regularly, as they are likely to swallow hairs when grooming themselves. These can ultimately cause a blockage in the stomach. The most obvious symptom of a so-called "fur ball" is that your cat becomes rather fussy about its food, eating smaller meals more often than in the past. Seek veterinary advice if you suspect this problem.

FELINE CHARACTERISTICS

For Feline Characteristics, see page 53

Full tail
The long, bushy tail looks very impressive when carried upright as the cat walks.

Tufted paws
The fur on the lower legs and paws is relatively short.

Light underparts
The distinctive ticking is concentrated on the head, back, and flanks, with the underparts paler.

Cat types for people who appreciate natural things in life, and are looking for adaptable and amenable pets.

Torbie and White

Working Cats

Although some beautiful cats have been created by careful selective breeding involving different breeds, many of the most distinctive and popular cats today owe their origins to mutations that have cropped up spontaneously in nonpedigree populations. These have since been bred selectively and transformed into recognized breeds. This is not to say that such cats are any healthier or more robust than other breeds. In fact, cats—whatever their origins—are generally free from the large number of congenital and inherited medical conditions that can afflict bloodlines in the case of pedigree dogs.

The characteristic that serves to link these partricular cats is their temperament. All those featured in this chapter are usually adaptable and amenable, settling into the home without any particular worries, although as usual, longhaired examples will need more grooming than their shorthaired cousins.

It might sound as if this group of cats could be fairly similar to look at, but in reality, there is a wide variance in appearance within members of this group, relating not just to their coats, but also the color of their eyes and even the shape of their ears. They are bred in a wide range of colors and patterns, too, in most cases, but their availability will differ, however, with some of these cats being far less commonly kept than others.

Chartreux

Silver Tabby

1. American Shorthair

In the early days of this breed, even nonpedigree cats could be registered in what was then the Domestic Shorthair category. This created a broad-based gene pool and ensured that a wide range of colors and patterns could be developed.

AT A GLANCE
- Friendly
- Exist in many forms
- Playful nature
- Easy-care coat

History

The name of the breed was changed in 1965, in order to emphasize its origins, bringing it in line alongside the British Shorthair (see page 46) and the European Shorthair (see page 108). Perhaps because of an underlying similarity in appearance between these different groups, all of which were originally descended from nonpedigree cats, American Shorthairs have not become widely known overseas. Nevertheless, they do have a strong following in North America, being popular with exhibitors and pet-seekers alike. Perhaps ironically, the first litter of kittens accepted as representing this breed were bred from a British Shorthair parent. Today, the breed has increased in size, with American Shorthairs slightly larger that their British counterparts.

Colors and patterns

Virtually all colors and varieties are recognized for show purposes in the case of this breed, although there are some differences, depending on the individual registration body. Classic (blotched) and mackerel (striped) tabbies have widespread recognition, whereas ticked and spotted forms in this case are not as widely accepted. Blotched tabby patterning as seen in the cat below is regarded as the traditional form of the breed, because so many of the early cats seen in the U.S. were tabbies.

FELINE CHARACTERISTICS		NOTES
Starting out	A breed resembling an ordinary domestic cat, but larger in size.	Was originally known for a period in its history as the Domestic Shorthair.
Personality	Well-balanced, friendly, and adaptable nature. Gets along well with people and dogs.	
Appearance	Powerfully built, relatively large cat, with an alert expression. Males are bigger.	Bred in a wide variety of colors and patterns.
At home	Settles in well, proving to be affectionate but does like to wander outdoors.	
Behavior	Likes to explore outdoors. Not a good choice as an indoor house cat.	
Grooming	Very straightforward. Occasional brushing and combing will be needed.	
Common health issues	Can be affected by the heart disease hypertrophic cardiomyopathy.	There is no cure for this condition, but medication can alleviate it.

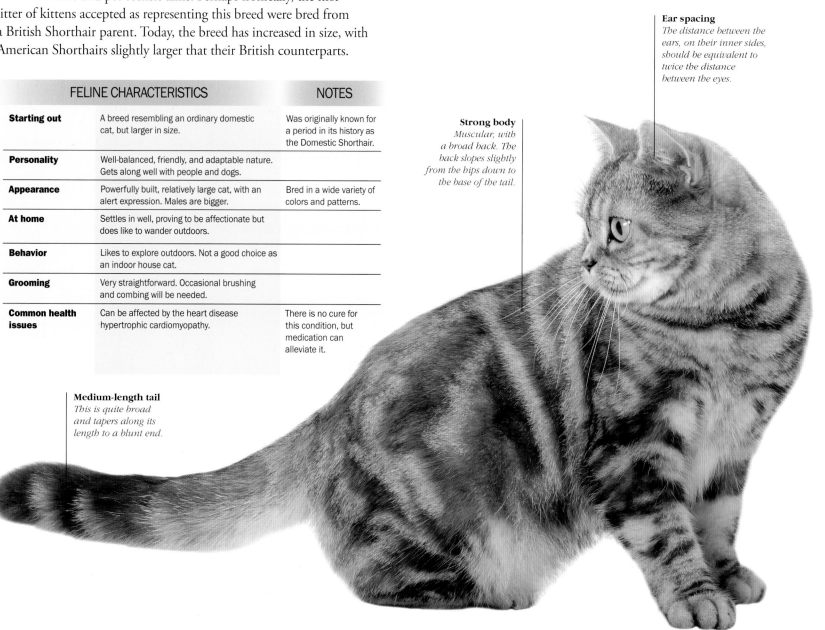

Ear spacing
The distance between the ears, on their inner sides, should be equivalent to twice the distance between the eyes.

Strong body
Muscular, with a broad back. The back slopes slightly from the hips down to the base of the tail.

Medium-length tail
This is quite broad and tapers along its length to a blunt end.

2. American Curl Longhair

The distinctive curling of their ears gives these cats a very unusual appearance, but their care is still straightforward. They are not disadvantaged in any way by their ears, and they make excellent companions, being tolerant, quiet, and affable by nature.

AT A GLANCE
- Unmistakable appearance
- Relaxed, quiet nature
- Good color choice
- Straightforward grooming

FELINE CHARACTERISTICS		NOTES
Starting out	A mutation that cropped up in domestic stray cats.	
Personality	Lively and responsive, settling in well to a domestic routine.	
Appearance	Medium-size, with both longhairs and shorthairs having a silky coat texture.	Bred in a wide range of colors and patterns.
At home	Make very good companions, being friendly and affectionate by nature.	
Behavior	Enjoy human company, often actively seeking attention.	
Grooming	Relatively straightforward, as they do not have a dense undercoat.	Even longhaired examples do not have particularly profuse coats.
Common health issues	None, in spite of their curled ears. These cause no problems.	Be careful that the ears are not hurt by children poking them.

History

It was back in 1981 that Californian couple Grace and Joe Ruga found two stray kittens outside their home. The couple offered food to their visitors, and before long, one of the cats had adopted them. She was black in color, with a long, silky coat, and ears that curled at their tips. The couple named her Shulamith, meaning "peaceful one." She ultimately gave birth to four kittens, two of which had similar ears, confirming that this was a dominant mutation. As a result, mating between an individual with curled ears and a normal cat will result in a percentage of their kittens also having curled ears, making it easier to develop this characteristic.

Care

In the longhaired form, there is very little undercoat, with the coat silky and sleek, lying close against the body. The grooming needs of these cats are therefore relatively minimal. As selective breeding has taken place, so the curling has been developed, to the extent that the ears may extend back almost to the skull. Young children must be supervised to ensure they drop nothing down the cat's ears or handle them roughly.

Slim body
The body is elongated and relatively narrow in shape.

Long face
The head shape of these cats is relatively long, compared with its width.

Plumed tail
The fur here is longer than elsewhere on the body.

3. American Wirehair

The unique wiry feel of the fur of these cats sets them apart and can affect the appearance of their coloration, too. Their distinctive coat is straightforward to take care of and needs no special care, although not everyone may appreciate its texture.

History

This breed's ancestry can be traced back to a kitten born in 1966 in upstate New York, as part of a litter of farm cats. The wirehaired kitten and one of his female littermates were obtained by a local cat breeder, with the aim of creating a wirehaired breed. It soon emerged that this characteristic was a dominant genetic trait, which made it easier to increase the numbers of such cats. When a cat of this type is paired with a cat with a normal coat, a percentage of wirehaired kittens should then result in the litter. Today, the breed still remains more common in North America than elsewhere, but only small numbers are registered each year. They are virtually unknown elsewhere.

Large eyes
Well spaced and round in shape.

Relatively large body
Males tend to grow to a bigger size than females.

FELINE CHARACTERISTICS		NOTES
Starting out	Very distinctive mutation, descended from a single individual.	Still rare today, and its distinctive coat does not appeal to everyone.
Personality	Typically resembles that of an ordinary domestic cat, being calm and inquisitive.	
Appearance	Springy, coarse-textured fur is characteristic of this breed. Medium size.	The long guard hairs, the secondary awn hairs, and the down are all curled.
At home	Happy roaming around home and yard. Does not like being confined indoors.	The origin of this breed was on a farm. Type of the cat has changed.
Behavior	Likes to investigate its environment and retains its hunting instincts.	
Grooming	Unusual coat requires relatively little grooming— other than stroking.	
Common health issues	These cats suffer no particular health problems and are quite hardy.	

Coat type

The hairs in the coat are not as thick as normal, and they are crimped or bent, with even the whiskers often curled. The coat can change significantly from kittenhood onward, so although it may appear coarse and dense early in life, this is no guarantee that it will retain these desirable features once it has matured. Conversely, a kitten whose coat may have appeared less satisfactory at that stage can develop a much more impressive appearance with age.

Wiry tail
The tail tapers along its length, with a rounded tip.

4. Chartreux

These beautiful blue cats are unfortunately quite scarce, but they make very friendly companions. The Chartreux probably represents Europe's oldest cat breed and is in part defined by its unique coloration. There are no other color variants of this breed.

AT A GLANCE

- Exotic breed history
- Unique coat
- Quiet, sometimes chirping
- Adaptable nature

History

The Chartreux (usually pronounced "shar-troo") is inextricably linked with the Grande Chartreuse monastery, located north of Grenoble in France. It has been suggested that its ancestors were feral cats living in the mountains of Syria, brought back to France in the 1200s by knights returning from the Crusades. A number of the Crusaders joined the Carthusian order, which might help explain how these cats could have found their way to the monastery. The Chartreux is an ancient breed, with the first description of the "blue cat" dating back to the 1700s and featured in the writings of the French naturalist Buffon. It was rescued from extinction at the end of World War II and then seen for the first time in the U.S. during 1971.

Breed features

The coat of these cats is very distinctive and not just in terms of coloration. It has a unique woolly texture, so that it actually feels like sheep's wool. It also has so-called "breaks," over the chest for example, where the fur parts naturally. This is largely the result of the dense undercoat, while the top coat is decidedly weather resistant. Simply stroking suffices to keep the coat in good condition. Chartreux grow to a large size and will mature slowly over two years, especially in the case of males, although they are remarkably agile cats and effective hunters.

Gold or copper eyes
These are a feature of the breed, although they are not as colorful in young or elderly cats.

Gender differences
Females in this case have a lighter build, and do not develop jowls on the face as they mature.

FELINE CHARACTERISTICS		NOTES
Starting out	A unique ancient breed, now associated with France and rare elsewhere.	History extends back to the Middle Ages, originating from Syria.
Personality	Sensitive cat, with a calm nature, proving very loyal and affectionate as well.	
Appearance	A breed defined by its coloration, which is blue, and its wool-like coat texture.	Powerfully built as well, with males having prominent jowls.
At home	Settles well, and is quiet. Engages in periods of robust play and then sleep.	
Behavior	Retains strong hunting instincts. Enthusiastic about food, and can easily become obese.	Learns by observation, in terms of opening doors, for example.
Grooming	Sheeplike coat really only needs stroking to keep the coat in good condition.	These cats used to be valued for their distinctive pelts.
Common health issues	No significant health problems have been reported in this breed.	

Tapering tail
The Chartreux's tail is thick at the base, tapering along its length.

5. European Shorthair

Although it is a relatively recent addition to the show scene, the ancestors of such cats have been kept in mainland Europe for millennia. As might be anticipated, these are loyal, affectionate cats that prefer to have some opportunity to roam outside.

History

There used to be a greater similarity between British and European Shorthairs, at a time when British Shorthairs (see page 46) were being used to aid the development of this breed, with a view to boosting its size. Since then, however, the cobby effect derived from British stock has been negated, with a ban on further crossbreeding of this type, but this has done nothing to raise the overall popularity of these cats. European Shorthairs are most popular in Scandinavian countries today but have struggled to obtain recognition elsewhere. This is almost certainly because they do look very similar to ordinary nonpedigree cats, especially when compared with many of the other more exotic breeds that are available.

Their appeal

Nevertheless, European Shorthairs are hardy and settle well in domestic surroundings. Signs of their working ancestry are reflected by their hunting instincts, however, which are still finely tuned today, whether seeking birds or rodents. They tend to get along well with other cats as well as dogs and are naturally friendly. There is also a wide choice of colors and patterns within the breed. A more recent trend—just as in the case of the British Shorthair— has been the development of colorpoint varieties within this group.

FELINE CHARACTERISTICS		NOTES
Starting out	Rather similar to an ordinary domestic cat but bigger in overall size.	Has not proved to be very popular outside of northern Europe.
Personality	Friendly, affable breed that has an adaptable nature.	Settles well in a home either with children or dogs.
Appearance	Looks very similar to a large domestic cat, with a powerful body.	
At home	Makes a good companion, but likely to be an effective hunter outdoors, too.	
Behavior	Home-loving but also wanders, being too active to be an indoor house cat.	
Grooming	Soft, short coat needs minimal grooming. Lies flat against the body.	
Common health issues	None of significance, proving to be hardy and long-lived in general.	Blue- or odd-eyed whites may be entirely or partly deaf.

Medium-size ears
These have slightly rounded tips and may be tufted in some cases.

Tabby rings
Alternating light and dark bands of fur present on the tail, which has a black tip.

Round paws
The paws are attached to sturdy, medium-size legs. The body is muscular and strong, but not cobby, distinguishing these cats from British Shorthairs.

6. German Rex

Several different Rex mutations have been reported in Germany since the 1930s, but genetic studies have shown this variety is very similar to the Cornish Rex (see page 59), bred in England. Friendly by nature, the German Rex is both playful and intelligent.

(see page 59)

AT A GLANCE

- Descended from a stray
- Traditional color is black
- Velvetlike fur
- Nearly became extinct

History

It was in 1951 that a doctor spotted an unusual black cat in the grounds of a hospital in Berlin-Buch. Further investigation revealed that the cat had been living there since 1947 and had bred previously. She became known as Lämmchen, which is the German word for "little lamb," and gave birth to a litter of three kittens in the doctor's care. All had normal coats, but then when the male was mated back to Lämmchen, two of the resulting four kittens displayed the same type of coat as their mother. Others followed, and the emerging breed then attracted considerable attention at the 1960 Paris Cat Club show, when it was seen in public for the first time. Unfortunately, this interest was not maintained for long.

Back from the brink

A number of the kittens were exported to the U.S., being crossed with Cornish Rexes, and by the time of Lämmchen's death, the breed was already very scarce. It had nearly disappeared completely by the late 1990s but was saved by the dedicated efforts of breeders in Germany and other parts of Europe. It may be that the Rex gene underlying this mutation is more widely distributed than previously thought, as odd individuals displaying this characteristic type of coat still crop up occasionally in feral populations of German cats. This offers hope to breeders seeking new outcrosses.

FELINE CHARACTERISTICS		NOTES
Starting out	A typically curly coated Rex breed originating in Germany back in the 1940s.	Nearly became extinct, but now undergoing a revival in parts of Europe.
Personality	Lively and intelligent, very interested in what is happening in its vicinity.	
Appearance	Slender legs, rounded face and large ears, with a short, silky textured, curly coat.	Even the whiskers usually display some signs of curling.
At home	Makes an ideal companion, not being excessively noisy yet generally affectionate.	
Behavior	Simply stoking the coat by hand should be adequate to maintain its condition.	
Grooming	Will relax when being picked up gently and petted. More nervous in strange surroundings.	Very similar mutation to the Cornish Rex, which arose in the U.K.
Common health issues	No significant breed-related health problems recorded in this case.	

Silky coat
The fur will tend to curl, although the whiskers are straighter than in the case of the Cornish Rex. The coat feels like velvet.

Long tail
This is of similar length to the body and quite slender.

Relatively heavy body
This more closely resembles that of the European Shorthair (see opposite) rather than that of the similar Cornish Rex mutation.

7. Scottish Fold

Whereas the American Curl mutation (see page 105) causes the ears to fold back, this mutation results in them falling forward over the head. All of today's Scottish Folds stem from a single female of this type, which in turn descended from a Scottish farm cat.

History

The breed's founder, christened Susie, was a shorthaired cat, but it soon became clear that she had been carrying the longhaired gene. This, in turn, means that, today, both coat types may be represented in a litter of Scottish Folds. The distinction between them is most apparent during the winter, when the coat of longhairs is most profuse. There will be a long brush of fur evident on the tails of the longhaired cats and a pronounced ruff of longer fur under the neck. Scottish Folds are not mated, though, as this can cause joint problems. Instead, cats from litters that resemble Scottish Folds in type, aside from the shape of their ears, are used to pair with them.

On the decline

Unfortunately, longhaired examples of the breed have become increasingly scarce, simply because the British Shorthair was the main established breed used as an outcross to develop the Scottish Fold. Since the longhaired characteristic is genetically recessive, this has meant that as the percentage of shorthaired genes has increased in the population, so the incidence of longhaired individuals being produced in litters has declined accordingly. These cats can be bred in any color or pattern, although not as colorpoints.

FELINE CHARACTERISTICS

For Feline Characteristics, see page 52

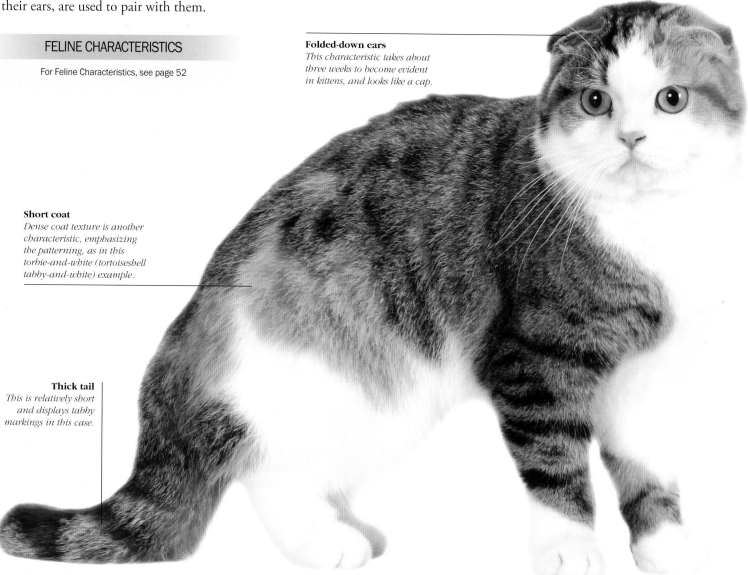

Folded-down ears
This characteristic takes about three weeks to become evident in kittens, and looks like a cap.

Short coat
Dense coat texture is another characteristic, emphasizing the patterning, as in this torbie-and-white (tortoiseshell tabby-and-white) example.

Thick tail
This is relatively short and displays tabby markings in this case.

8. Kurelian Bobtail

Named after the remote Kuril Islands, an archipelago extending around 750 miles (1,200 km) from the eastern coast of Russia down toward Japan, this distinctive breed has only recently become known elsewhere in the world, having lived in the region for centuries.

AT A GLANCE

- Highly distinctive breed
- Has developed naturally
- Still relatively unknown
- Occurs in two coat types

Large head
Very broad head, with a relatively wide muzzle, plus a straight nose and rounded chin.

Tabby patterning
Markings of this type are common, reinforcing the breed's "wild type" appearance.

Powerful legs
The hind legs are slightly longer than the front legs.

History

There are 56 islands in this group, with the majority being uninhabited. As to when the ancestors of the cats arrived, this is unclear. They could possibly have been abandoned by visiting ships, which was not uncommon when cats were always carried as a means of controlling rodent populations. The bobtail characteristic is well documented in cat populations throughout Asia, and it is known that this breed is unrelated to the Japanese bobtail (see page 130), which is the most obvious candidate to have contributed to its ancestry. It is therefore most likely, given the location, that Kurelian Bobtails evolved naturally in isolation, from introduced cats brought from mainland Asia. They then adapted to life on the islands over many generations. This gave rise to the distinctive breed of today.

Unique features

The coat of the Kurelian Bobtail is flat, quite long, and weather resistant, reflecting the relatively harsh climate of the region. For show purposes, both shorthaired and semi-longhaired versions of the breed are recognized, with the tails of the latter being longer, measuring up to 5 in. (13cm) in length. The number of vertebrae in the tail can vary, but there will be at least two discernible here. These cats are very active and retain strong hunting instincts, being able to catch fish very effectively.

FELINE CHARACTERISTICS		NOTES
Starting out	Originates from remote islands off the coast of mainland Asia.	Breed is now represented in a number of different countries worldwide.
Personality	Gentle by nature and sociable, reputed to live in groups in its natural habitat.	
Appearance	Relatively square body shape when seen in profile, although the hindquarters are slightly taller.	
At home	Not a breed to keep confined in the home, as its instinct is to explore.	
Behavior	Unusual calls that sound more like the trilling of a bird than those of a cat.	Generally produces small litters of two or three kittens.
Grooming	Straightforward brushing and combing will be adequate.	
Common health issues	None recorded. They do not suffer health problems linked to the bobtail.	

9. Ojos Azules

These particular cats are unique, being bred and named as a result of their eye coloration. They are currently low in numbers, and their future is still very uncertain. Not all would-be breeds actually become established and thrive, for a variety of reasons.

AT A GLANCE
- Stunning eye color
- Very rare breed
- Easy-care coat
- Friendly nature

History

Ojos Azules is a Spanish name and literally means "blue eyes," referring to the main distinguishing feature of these cats, which has attracted breeders to them. Here, for the first time, is a cat that has dark blue eyes but is neither white in color, nor a colorpoint variety. Deep, rich blue coloration is preferred, and this characteristic can be seen in any Ojos Azules, irrespective of its coloration. The breed's origins can be traced back to Cornflower, who was a tortoiseshell cat found in New Mexico back in 1984. In some cases, as shown here, only one of the eyes may be blue. This condition is described as heterochromia, with the other eye being green, gold, or copper.

Appearance

White individuals are not encouraged in this breed, because it is difficult to distinguish between them and ordinary blue-eyed white cats, which are likely to be deaf. As a result, patches of color are encouraged, particularly on the extremities of the body, with the color of the eyes being regulated by an independent dominant gene. The coat itself is short and silky. In terms of their overall appearance, Ojos Azules are intermediate between the cobby shape of many shorthaired breeds and the svelte outline of Oriental breeds like the Siamese (see page 86).

Rounded forehead
The overall head shape should correspond to that of an equilateral triangle.

Large eyes
These are rounded in appearance, emphasizing this breed feature.

Pointed tail
The tail tip of Ojos Azules should always be white in color.

FELINE CHARACTERISTICS		NOTES
Starting out	A relatively new yet still rare breed, originating in the southern U.S.	
Personality	Affectionate and lively by nature, being eager to explore indoors and out.	
Appearance	Distinguished and named after the deep, cornflower-blue coloration of its eyes.	Can occur with any coat color, allowing nonpointed blue-eyed cats to be bred.
At home	Typically friendly breed, descended from nonpedigree ancestral stock.	
Behavior	Eager to play, and settles well in the home, due to its adaptable nature.	
Grooming	Coat care is easy. Even longhaired cats do not have a dense undercoat.	
Common health issues	To avoid stillbirths, Ojos Azules must be mated with other cats, not each other.	

10. Longhaired Selkirk Rex

Most breeds originating from working cat roots have increased in size, as the result of crossings with purebred cats, with the Selkirk Rex no exception. This has also led in this case to the development of a longhaired form.

AT A GLANCE

- Highly distinctive coat
- Relatively large breed
- Daily grooming needed
- Bred in any form

History

Outcrossing to Persians led to the creation of this longhaired form of the Selkirk Rex. The primary aim of using Persians was to increase the length of the hair, and thereby emphasize the impact of the curling evident in the coat, but it has also increased the range of color varieties. Chocolate coloration, as displayed by this individual, was probably introduced in this way. The natural "look" of the breed can be ruined, however, by excessive grooming, causing the longer fur to appear straighter than would otherwise be the case. A similar effect can occur if the coat becomes wet, and exhibitors have to allow several days following a bath for the naturally springy, curly nature of the coat to be restored, in order for the cat to look its best for exhibition purposes.

Distinguishing characteristics

The longhaired gene was carried by the founder of this breed, which was evolved in Montana. In true Rex style, these cats were named after a geographical locality—in this case, the Selkirk Mountains—but what sets them apart from other rexes is that the long guard hairs in their coat are not reduced in length or missing. Instead, they are simply curled. Another key difference is that they will regularly shed their hairs, and so cannot be considered a hypoallergenic breed. Playful and cuddly, both longhaired and shorthaired (see page 75) Selkirk Rexes make excellent companions, and are very popular in many countries.

FELINE CHARACTERISTICS

For Feline Characteristics, see page 75

Coat quality
Neutering of both males and females usually improves the quality of the coat.

Plush coat
The curls are usually most evident along the flanks, extending to the underside of the body, and on the neck, too.

Thick tail
Has distinctive curls along its length and ends in a rounded tip.

Cat types for people who have a taste for the exotic and expensive, with some of the newer breeds covered that command very high prices.

Safari

Wild Cats

The most recognizable trend in cat breeding during the late twentieth century was the creation of new breeds displaying stunning markings, and interest in this field has continued into the new millennium. Some of these cats, like the Ocicat, have been created by using existing breeds. Following the emergence of the Bengal, however, with its distinctive patterning, other breeders (especially in North America) have sought to mate different species of wild cat with domestic cats for this purpose.

This process is far less straightforward than simply mating two existing breeds of domestic cat, however, and not just because of the potentially aggressive behavior of the wild cat. The difficulty surrounds mating species that are not that closely related. Although this can lead to the production of hybrid offspring, the likelihood is that such kittens may be infertile. The influence of the wild cat is minimal after the initial mating, however, with the aim simply being to transfer the desired coat characteristics across into the domestic bloodlines. This is usually achieved by pairing a male wild cat to a female domestic cat, simply because it is considerably easier to manage a pregnant domestic cat through what initially may be a difficult birth.

Another issue is the lack of availability of wild cat sires, not to mention legislation in some countries that would make pairings of this type almost impossible to accomplish. But as the Bengal has shown, the results can be a stunning addition to the list of breeds that are available.

Sokoke

1. Ashera

This is currently said to be one of the newest hybrid breeds, and as such, is very rare. The Ashera is also especially controversial because of the debate about its origins. However, there is no doubting the striking patterning of these cats, nor their large size.

AT A GLANCE

• Mired in controversy

• Very large

• Exceedingly expensive

• Origins open to doubt

History

The Ashera is reputedly a combination of crosses featuring both the African Serval (*Leptailurus serval*) and the Asian Leopard Cat (*Prionailurus bengalensis*), mated with domestic cats. Asheras were originally sold by a Delaware-based biotechnology company with the stated aim of breeding hypoallergenic cats. A breeder based in Pennsylvania challenged this assertion, however, claiming that several so-called Asheras sent to the Netherlands were simply first-generation Savannah (see page 124) crosses, being sold without his knowledge. The kittens in question were seized on arrival, and DNA tests were then carried out. In the case of these particular cats, it was confirmed that they were the result of mating between a Savannah and an Egyptian Mau (see page 61).

Individual markings
The barring and spotting on the legs especially is highly individual.

Large head
These cats will dwarf ordinary domestic cats, potentially weighing about 40 lbs. (18 kg).

Spotted patterning
This is very similar to that of the Egyptian Mau, suggesting the Ashera is a hybrid being developed using this breed.

FELINE CHARACTERISTICS		NOTES
Starting out	A hybrid breed with a recent wild cat input.	Controversial, with disputed origins.
Personality	Depends on the individual's proximity to the original wild cat, in generational terms.	Those further removed, with a higher percentage of domestic cat input will be tamer.
Appearance	Much bigger than a domestic cat, with an exotic spotted appearance.	Can stand 3.3 ft. (1 m) tall on their hind legs, giving them considerable reach.
At home	Can be shy and withdrawn, also likely to be more active than a domestic cat.	
Behavior	May display strong hunting instincts, and is able to jump and climb very effectively.	
Grooming	Sleek, short coat that needs little grooming. Stroking will often suffice.	
Common health issues	None has been recorded as yet in this case.	

A reality check

The Savannah itself was bred from a Serval parent at the outset, so there would be a similarity in appearance between an Ashera and a Savannah. The finding in the Dutch case does not preclude a breeding program as originally described, though, but certainly, this affair has cast a serious question mark over the Ashera's validity as a breed that has had any input from Asian Leopard Cats. The problem is that the cost of such cats runs into tens of thousands of dollars, providing plenty of scope for unscrupulous breeders.

2. Bengal

By far the best known of the hybrid cat breeds, the Bengal has become very popular over recent years, thanks to its stunning appearance, which is quite unlike that of any other breed. These cats are friendly, as well as athletic by nature.

AT A GLANCE

- Striking patterning
- Snow Bengals are born white
- Not averse to bathing
- Satin-textured coat

FELINE CHARACTERISTICS		NOTES
Starting out	Stunningly attractive; large cat with an athletic nature.	Litterbox training is not always easy.
Personality	Demands attention, but definitely not a lap cat. Can be quite independent.	
Appearance	Can display a spotted or marbled appearance, which should be horizontal.	Males are larger than females, weighing up to 18 lbs. (8 kg).
At home	Not well suited to a small apartment, as these cats are active and need space.	
Behavior	Very playful and often lethal hunters. Quiet nature.	
Grooming	Brushing and combing once a week should be sufficient for this shorthaired breed.	Coat patterning tends to become less evident during molting periods.
Common health issues	Can be vulnerable to kidney problems and the heart disorder hypertrophic cardiomyopathy (HCM).	

History

Back in 1963, a geneticist named Jean Sugden bred an Asian Leopard Cat (*Felis bengalensis*) with a domestic cat, but circumstances prevented her from pursuing her interest in this field. The initial development of the Bengal began not as an attempt to create a new breed of cat, but as a means of investigating Feline Leukemia Virus (FeLV). In due course, some of these hybrids passed into the care of Jean Sugden, who had remarried and was now Jean Mill. She then started a careful breeding program, based around pairing these hybrids with domestic cats, including both Egyptian Maus (see page 61) and nonpedigree shorthairs. This ensured that the offspring over successive generations became much more friendly, but it did not affect their stunning appearance.

Colors and patterns

Both spotted and marbled patterns are associated with the breed, with spotting the most common. There should be a glittery effect over the coat, and the markings must be clearly defined. The marbled pattern is very distinctive and does not correspond to that of the classic blotched tabby. Two basic color variants are recognized. Brown Bengals can vary in terms of coloration from gray shades to deep red, while the white or snow form with seal patterning may have blue eyes, although odd-eyed individuals also occur.

Large cat
Bengals are bigger than a typical domestic cat and powerfully built.

Thick tail
This is normally carried low when the cat is walking, like a wild cat.

Tabby markings
Barring is to be seen on the legs, with the coat thick and having a luxurious feel.

3. Californian Spangled

It was a chance encounter with a leopard in Africa that led to the development of this breed. The Californian Spangled was intended as a symbol to highlight the plight of the world's wild cat populations, being specifically created for this purpose.

AT A GLANCE

- Mini wild cat
- Distinctive appearance
- Friendly, playful nature
- A rare breed

History

Hollywood scriptwriter Paul Casey wanted to develop a breed that not only looked like a wild cat, but also moved in a similar way. He established a complex breeding program that extended over a decade, using a variety of purebred and nonpedigree cats from around the world. They included street cats from Malaysia and Egypt, and breeds including Abyssinians, seal-point Siamese, Manx, and British Shorthairs. Even the launch of this new breed was carefully planned to ensure maximum publicity, with the breed featuring on the cover of one of the most famous U.S. Christmas catalogs. In another inspired move, Paul named all his cats after Native American tribes, guaranteeing further interest in their origins.

Colors

A range of different colors was created, including bronze, gold, blue, red, and silver, with the spotted patterning clearly defined. It was never Paul Casey's intention to develop a cat primarily for show purposes, however, and in fact, his aim was to ensure that the breed maintained a rather exclusive image. Only a few cats were exported outside the U.S., and following Paul's death in 2007, it appears that its numbers have now fallen significantly, to the point where ironically, its own future survival may be under threat.

FELINE CHARACTERISTICS		NOTES
Starting out	A rare domestic cat, bred from both nonpedigree and purebred stock.	Created primarily as an emblem of the conservation movement.
Personality	Very friendly, loyal cats that thrive on human company.	
Appearance	Low slung; resembles a miniature leopard in terms of style and substance.	Spotted coat, with large whisker pads that highlight the cheek bones.
At home	Very playful and enjoy chasing after or leaping to catch toys.	
Behavior	Athletic nature and very lively, especially as kittens. Enthusiastic in terms of jumping.	Possess sharp and often lethal hunting skills, too.
Grooming	Straightforward, due to their short coat, Markings may fade when molting.	
Common health issues	None recorded in this breed, which had an incredibly varied ancestry.	

Long, muscular body
This particular feature emphasizes the breed's leopardlike appearance, reinforced by its low-slung gait.

Range of spots
These do not have to be circular but can be in a range of different shapes, including ovals and even triangles.

Well-sculpted cheekbones
This adds to the "wild" image associated with the breed, as do the ears, which are set back from the face.

4. Chausie

These cats are surprisingly variable in size, depending on their origins, and have started to become popular. Although good-natured, they are demanding, thanks to their natural intelligence and ability to climb, run, and hunt effectively. Their grooming needs, however, are minimal.

AT A GLANCE

- Large breed
- Matures slowly
- Three recognizable varieties
- Athletic nature

History

The origins of the Chausie extend back to the 1960s, although only during recent years, thanks to the rising popularity of the Bengal, has the breed come to prominence. The initial aim was to create a domestic breed that looked like the Jungle Cat (*Felis chaus*) but had a far more tractable and friendly disposition. This species occurs over a very wide area from Turkey eastward to Malaysia, with these cats also occurring in Egypt. Although considered to be the largest member of the *Felis* genus, they do vary significantly, both in size and coloration, through their range. This is now reflected in the case of the Chausie, whose weight can vary from 15–30 lbs. (6.8–13.6kg).

Development

The Abyssinian (see page 44) breed played a significant part in the development of the Chausie, thanks to its ticked tabby appearance. There is also a solid black form of the Chausie, plus a black grizzled-tabby form, where the background color is dark, and there is white banding in the center of individual hairs, with the tips black. Inherited from the Jungle Cat, this patterning is only seen in this breed. These cats are very active and should only be kept where they have space to exercise.

FELINE CHARACTERISTICS		NOTES
Starting out	A wild cat hybrid, but less popular than spotted members of this group.	
Personality	Depends on how far removed the cat is from its wild cat ancestor.	The fourth generation (F4) will be quite tractable and less nervous.
Appearance	Large cat often with a ticked tabby coat. Males are larger than females.	The Abyssinian breed has contributed significantly to the Chausie's development.
At home	Very agile, being able to leap almost 6 ft. (1.8 m) vertically on occasions.	
Behavior	Confident, intelligent, and loves to play. Has a curious nature.	Takes up to 3 years to attain adult size.
Grooming	Minimal grooming required, due to the short coat of these cats.	
Common health issues	Some individuals display gluten intolerance and this must be reflected in their diet.	

Large, wide ears
These are prominent in this breed and are sometimes tufted. The head looks similar to that of a mini cougar.

White chin
This is a feature of the Jungle Cat, although white areas here are not uncommon in the Abyssinian, either.

Deep chest
With the body itself muscular and long.

5. Ocicat

The Ocicat is a breed that came about by chance, but it has since become very popular as a pet. This is not just thanks to the stylish good looks of these cats, but also as a result of their appealing, playful personality.

History

A breeder in Michigan named Victoria Daly was attempting to breed Siamese with points matching the appearance of an Abyssinian. One of the kittens that ultimately resulted was spotted and looked like an Ocelot (*Leopardus pardalis*), and so was dubbed an Ocicat. He was neutered, but the pairing was repeated, to see if any further such cats could be produced. Luckily, the quest was successful, and so the development of the breed began. Outcrossings to American Shorthairs helped increase its size, and the range of available colors, but it was not until just over 20 years later, in 1986, that these cats started to become recognized for show purposes. A similar breeding program begun later in Europe saw a separate Ocicat bloodline develop there.

FELINE CHARACTERISTICS		NOTES
Starting out	Attractively patterned, medium-size breed, with individual patterning.	Quite lively by nature.
Personality	Playful cat that enjoys human company. Friendly, affectionate nature.	
Appearance	Distinctive spotted patterning with barring on the lower parts.	Clear contrast needed between background coat color and the markings.
At home	Calm but active nature and will climb or jump up onto furniture readily.	Generally settles well in the company of a dog.
Behavior	Will actively seek out attention; jumps and climbs quite readily. Quite vocal.	
Grooming	Weekly brushing and combing should suffice in this case.	
Common health issues	Watch the dental health of these cats, as they are susceptible to tartar.	

Prominent eye markings
The mascara lines extending out from the eyes must be clearly defined, as here.

Individual patterns
The spotted patterning on the body, and the barring on the limbs, is an individual feature.

Appearance

These cats are relatively large, well-built, and muscular, with males bigger and heavier than females. There are three colors recognized, in the guise of chocolate, cinnamon, and tawny (which is the brown form), and dilute forms of these as well—blue, lilac, and fawn. The spotted patterning in the case of the dilute varieties is less pronounced, though, thanks to the dilution effect. There are also silver forms of each of these colors, with the white ground color emphasizing the patterning.

Black tail
The tip of the tail serves to indicate the cat's color, with the remainder of the tail encircled with alternating light and dark rings.

6. Safari

The Safari is another very rare wild cat hybrid that was actually created before the Bengal, but has never attained its level of popularity. Nevertheless, there are signs that this cat is now beginning to be bred more commonly today.

FELINE CHARACTERISTICS		NOTES
Starting out	One of the rarest breeds of hybrid origins. Unknown outside North America.	Bred from Geoffroy's Cat crossed with American Shorthairs and Bengals.
Personality	Said to be friendlier, even in the initial generations, than many such hybrids.	
Appearance	Relatively long-legged with a slim body, with spotted and barred markings.	Various color variants have been created.
At home	Calm but active nature; will climb or jump up onto furniture readily.	
Behavior	Often eager to hunt and hardy by nature. Will climb trees readily.	
Grooming	Brushing will help reinforce the attractive coat patterning.	
Common health issues	Males of early generations are usually infertile, but females can give birth.	Infertility lasts until the fourth generation (F4).

Breeding outcomes

Interestingly, although Geoffroy's Cat tends to be smaller than the typical domestic cat, hybridization has resulted in offspring that are larger than either of the founder breeds. This is sometimes described as hybrid vigor, with adult Safari cats typically weighing around 25 lbs. (11.3 kg) in the case of males and 18 lbs. (8.1 kg) for females in the first generation (often abbreviated to F1). The young born over subsequent generations become smaller again, when they are mated with domestic cats.

History

The origins of these cats lie in the same research program investigating the Feline Leukemia Virus that ultimately resulted in the breeding of the Bengal (see page 117). In this case, though, the Geoffroy's Cat (*Leopardus geoffroyi*), a wild species which is widely distributed in parts of Central and South America, was mated with domestic cats. Once again, the coloration of these cats differs widely through their range, and this is reflected to some extent in the Safari breed today. It began in 1970, but the problem of chromosomal differences between the Geoffroy's Cat and domestic cats was a major handicap—this, in fact, triggered interest in the Bengal breeding program instead. But as the Bengal became popular as a pet, so attention then switched back to this original pairing.

Large breed
F1 crosses are large, but are said to be much friendlier than other similar crosses carried out using other types of wild cat.

Powerful hind legs
Safari cats are able to run and jump well as a result.

Spotted patterning
This is a breed characteristic, seen here in this dark-colored individual. Other lighter colors exist.

7. Toyger

The intention in this case is to create a cat that looks like a miniature tiger, with striped patterning on the sides of its body. This is such a distinctive and striking breed that it is almost guaranteed to become internationally popular.

AT A GLANCE

- Tigerlike stripes
- Affectionate nature
- Striking appearance
- Bred from domestic bloodlines

Rounded ears
These are well spaced and located toward the back of the head, with a dense covering of fur over them.

Well-spaced eyes
These should have a slight almond shape and need to be a rich, deep color.

Long tail
Fairly narrow and not tapering significantly along its length, ending in a blunt, round tip.

History

The development of this breed has been pioneered by Jean Mill, who also developed the Bengal (see page 117). The quest started back in the 1980s, working with mackerel tabby patterning. She managed to find a street cat which she imported from Kashmir, with a spotted patterning between the ears which normally display no patterning. She hoped that this feature could be used to create tigerlike stripes over successive generations, with the spots effectively merging to form stripes. Bengals have also been used to contribute to the developing bloodline, introducing both attractive coloration and their stunning fur quality, and perhaps most significantly, a larger body. The development of the Toyger is still continuing, and it is starting to attract more interest in show circles today, especially having obtained full Championship status in 2007.

Looking ahead

Future plans to show the ultimate desired appearance of the Toyger have already been mapped out, with the use of computer imaging assisting in the development of a cat breed probably for the first time. The Toyger is also becoming highly sought-after as a pet, thanks not just to its attractive lines, but also because of its delightful temperament. There is none of the shyness that can be found in early generations of wild cat hybrids.

FELINE CHARACTERISTICS		NOTES
Starting out	The result of crossbreeding between Bengals and mackerel tabbies.	Striking appearance has seen the breed becoming popular in Europe, too.
Personality	Well-adjusted, friendly cats, with an intelligent nature, settling well in the home.	
Appearance	A cat that resembles a miniature tiger with striped patterning.	Distinctive facial shape developed to resemble that of a tiger.
At home	Active temperament means they are too lively to be kept permanently indoors.	
Behavior	Lively, playful nature, and eager to join in with family activities.	
Grooming	Brushing keeps the coat looking immaculate, emphasizing the patterning.	Coat tends to display a silvery sheen, as well as a high gloss.
Common health issues	No significant issues. Not nervous either, unlike recent hybrid breeds.	

8. Cheetoh

This breed is another recent development, created in part from the Bengal (see page 117), but it has no direct wild cat genes in its ancestry. The aim has been to create a domestic spotted breed of cat that looks and moves like a cheetah (*Acinonyx jubatus*).

AT A GLANCE

- Wild cat style
- Range of colors
- Being developed universally
- Friendly nature

History

Cheetohs are the result of crossbreeding in the early 2000s between Bengals and a pure domestic breed, in the guise of the Ocicat (see page 120). These pairings, combined with careful selection, have led to the prominent spotted patterning of the Bengal being combined with the relatively long-legged appearance of the Ocicat, a trait derived from its Siamese ancestry. The resulting Cheetohs are surprisingly large, being significantly heavier than their ancestral breeds. Males may vary from 15–23 lbs. (6.8–10.4 kg), whereas females can weigh as much as 15 lbs. (6.8 kg). These cats have a very distinct style of movement, slouching like a true wild cat, combined with an athletic, lithe appearance. Cheetohs also have an unusually plush yet short coat with a velvety texture. In spite of their looks, however, the aim is to ensure that these cats retain their very friendly natures.

FELINE CHARACTERISTICS		NOTES
Starting out	Domestic cat with a wild cat look, based on a cheetah.	Ancestral breeds widely kept, so Cheetohs are internationally available.
Personality	Friendly, dependable nature, thriving on being part of the family.	Do not be fooled by the wild cat appearance in this particular case.
Appearance	Wild cat look. Eyes can be bronze, gold, copper, green-brown, or hazel in color.	The colorpointed form has characteristic blue eyes.
At home	Quite active by nature, this breed is not best suited to living permanently outside.	
Behavior	Males are exceedingly tolerant toward their kittens.	
Grooming	Brushing and combing will be needed about once a week or so.	Patterning may become less distinctive during periods of shedding.
Common health issues	None recorded, but kidney problems inherited from the Bengal could be an issue.	

Stunning coat
The sleek nature of the coat reinforces the athletic, lithe profile of this breed and also has an attractive, glossy quality.

Patterning
Well-defined pattern of individual markings, with the extent of the contrast in the coat varying somewhat, depending on the background color. The spots may be seen on the underside of the body, too.

Colors

The following varieties are among those recognized by breeders. There are both black/brown spotted sienna and tan variants, with tan (gold) Cheetohs displaying the lighter background color. There are also black spotted smoke and silver forms, with the latter being brighter, and displaying greater contrast between the background color and pattern. A lynx (tabby) pointed gold spotted snow form, whose body color is essentially snow white, broken by golden spots and rosettes, with the extremities being darker, has also been created. A pattern of black rings encircles the tail, confirming the lynx (tabby) influence here.

Broad tip
This tapers along its length and is likely to display typical tabby barring, usually ending in a dark tip.

9. Savannah

This breed is now considered to be the largest form of domestic cat in the world, with its size reflecting that of its African Serval ancestor. Its size alone means that this is a breed that should not be acquired without very considerable thought.

AT A GLANCE

- Striking appearance
- Distinctive patterning
- Large hybrid breed
- Chirps, purrs, and hisses

Tall ears
These are large and erect, mirroring those of the Serval, which has acute hearing, able to detect rodents out of sight in grassland areas.

Mixed markings
The ground color can vary from silver to amber, broken by a series of black stripes and spots.

Tail talk
Savannahs are known to wag their tails, similar to dogs, to greet their owners.

History

The Savannah was originally created by Judee Frank, a Bengal breeder, back in 1986. She successfully crossed a male Serval (*Leptailurus serval*) with a Siamese. Crossings of this type often result in kittens being born too early, however, because the Serval's gestation period is about ten days longer than that of a domestic cat. Even if the young are born successfully and survive, the F1 (first generation) males will be infertile, while both sexes will display strong wild cat tendencies, making them a potential liability. Progressive breeding from this point on with domestic cats will improve the temperament of the Savannah over successive generations. Once F4 is reached, however, these young Savannahs should be quite tractable and easily handled.

The evolving breed

It is likely to take another generation before a Savannah male is likely to be fertile, although both sexes can be shown from F3 onward. The aim of breeders has been to maintain key features of the Serval's attractive appearance, such as its long neck, legs, and short, attractively-marked coat, while ensuring that they are suitable pets, too, with friendly natures. It is especially important to socialize these cats from an early age. When grown, they are likely to weigh 18–30 lbs. (8.2–13.6 kg), with males heavier than females.

FELINE CHARACTERISTICS		NOTES
Starting out	Relatively large wild cat hybrid, bred from the Serval crossed with domestic cats.	Servals have actually been kept as pets, especially in their homelands.
Personality	Described as being rather doglike, even to the extent of walking on a leash.	
Appearance	Strongly influenced by the domestic cat breed used. Typically spotted.	
At home	May bounce at people as an unexpected way of greeting them.	
Behavior	Active and extrovert by nature. Can jump well and wags its tail in greeting.	Socialization is particularly important with these large cats.
Grooming	Simply brushing the coat will keep it in good condition.	
Common health issues	Liver size sometimes smaller than in other cats. May affect drug dosages.	Anesthetic ketamine may not be well tolerated.

10. Serengeti

In spite of its name, this breed has no links with Africa. It is so-called because of its similarity to a Serval, although it has been created in a totally separate breeding program, compared with the Savannah (see opposite).

(see opposite)

AT A GLANCE

- A domestic breed
- Wild cat appearance
- Striking markings
- Good household pet

FELINE CHARACTERISTICS		NOTES
Starting out	An interbreed cross, between Bengals and Orientals.	The aim is to produce a cat resembling a small Serval in appearance.
Personality	Active natures, and can be quite vocal on occasions, but very friendly, too.	
Appearance	Distinctively long-legged, with very large, rounded ears. Black spotted coat.	Self (solid) black—so-called "melanistic"—examples are known.
At home	Proves exceedingly playful, and should always have a good choice of toys.	
Behavior	Confident, with a dependable temperament. Can get along well with dogs.	
Grooming	Sleek coat with little undercoat results in minimal grooming needs.	
Common health issues	No significant problems have been recorded in this emergent breed.	

History

The creation of the Serengeti was conceived by Karen Sausman of the Kingsmark Cattery, in California. It is a relatively recent breeding project, with its origins dating back to 1994. Rather than following a hybridization program involving a wild cat, she carried out crosses between the Bengal breed (see page 117) and Orientals (see page 63) to achieve the goal of creating a miniature Serval-like cat. There are no associated problems with fertility or temperament of the young cats, and given the widespread availability of these founder breeds in the cat world, enthusiasts in other countries such as the U.K. have also started similar breeding programs. Various forms of the Serengeti are already recognized for show purposes, notably brown-spotted tabby, self-colored (solid) black, and both silver and smoke forms of ebony.

(see page 117) and Orientals (see page 63)

Well-defined patterning
There should be good contrast evident between the spots and the ground color, with the chin, muzzle, and underparts white.

Large, tall ears
These are wide and correspond to the length of the head in height and must be rounded at their tips.

The future

Breeders in the U.K. are also developing what will be a snow-spotted version, with this pattern deriving from the Bengal. Although males of the emerging Serengeti breed are bigger than females, they are still no heavier than half the weight of a Savannah, making them far more easily handled. Basically, the type (appearance) of the Serengeti has been derived from its Oriental ancestor, while its patterning tends to result from the Bengal input into its genetic make-up. In terms of temperament, they are confident, active, and playful cats. They will settle well in domestic surroundings, even in the company of a dog.

Long legs
These give the cat its characteristic height and terminate in oval, medium-size feet.

Cat types for people seeking not just a companion, but also a cat that is very likely to learn how to do things around the home.

Tortoiseshell

Talented Cats

All cats are, of course, talented, but it appears that some breeds may instinctively learn how to do things more readily than others, whether is it opening a cupboard door with a paw, walking on a harness, or even learning to retrieve a ball during the course of a game. Much depends on the individual, but as predators, cats must be adaptable.

Perhaps unsurprisingly, young cats learn more readily than adults, so you are more likely to find that you can teach your pet successfully at this stage than later in life. This reflects the way in which they are taught by their mother and is similar to the way in which young wild cats learn how to hunt and gain essential survival skills in the period just before and after weaning.

It is often said that ordinary, nonpedigree cats will prove to be the most adaptable, in terms of their learning skills. Other breeds that are descended from similar origins also display this type of character. In contrast, those such as Persian Longhairs, which have been pampered over the course of centuries—being reared in the confines of catteries over the course of many generations rather than roaming free—are the least likely to display such talents.

In addition, Asian breeds such as the Siamese, which are very focused on people, can also prove to be talented, with an almost telepathic bond, that is more likely to be a reflection of watching their owners' routines and interacting accordingly. Their natural agility helps as well, when they learn how to play games.

Torbie and White

1. Abyssinian

These attractive cats are very people-centric, forming a close bond with their owners and proving to be very affectionate. They have a very playful nature, and an individual will often play and sleep with the dog that shares the household, especially if they have grown up together.

AT A GLANCE
- Playful disposition
- Attentive nature
- Attractive appearance
- Very affectionate

FELINE CHARACTERISTICS

For Feline Characteristics, see page 44

Dark borders
The eyes have black inner lids, which highlight the eyes.

Medium body
The Abyssinian's profile is neither as cobby as that of one of the recognized shorthaired breeds, nor as svelte as that of a Siamese.

Blue coloration
Slate blue-and-beige banding extends down the hairs, with the underparts paler.

History

It is the range of breeds that contributed to the Abyssinian's development that have helped shape its intelligent, responsive personality. The breed was basically founded from just a single individual, and since then, a host of different crosses were used to maintain its distinctive appearance as a ticked tabby. Breeders have also removed tabby barring on the legs, which is a feature associated with other ticked tabby breeds, by selective breeding. This has given the Abyssinian—or "Aby," as it is often described—a unique appearance. One particular feature that is sought-after by breeders is ear tufts, which create a very different, exotic appearance, although these tend to be less evident now than in the past, possibly because of crossbreeding that has led to the development of other colors.

Ball play

Although Abyssinians are relatively quiet cats, they are far from unresponsive—quite the reverse. They delight in human company and can quite easily be trained to bring back a lightweight ball as part of a game. A wooden floor will be ideal for this purpose, because the ball will run freely over the surface here, encouraging the cat to chase after the ball and pat it with its feet. An Abyssinian is soon likely to learn to play like this on its own, occupying itself when you are elsewhere.

2. Havana Brown

These cats, although recognized as a separate breed, were actually the first of the Oriental varieties to be created. They were originally called the Chestnut Brown Foreign in England, becoming known as Havana Browns in North America.

AT A GLANCE

- Attractive brown coloration
- Sleek appearance
- Expressive nature
- Tactile

FELINE CHARACTERISTICS		NOTES
Starting out	Attractive distinctive brown coloration, with stunning eyes.	Not as readily available today as in the past.
Personality	Lively, active nature. Appreciates human company.	
Appearance	Svelte, sleek ,and elegant appearance, emphasizing its athletic nature.	
At home	Will seek to climb and jump, so be careful with items that could be knocked down.	
Behavior	Highly affectionate, and quite an extrovert nature, demanding attention.	Can be a sharp hunter, especially of birds.
Grooming	Very little grooming required, due to the smooth nature of the coat.	Simply stroking the coat helps contribute to its shiny appearance.
Common health issues	Can be at risk from respiratory infections and feels the cold.	Do not encourage these cats to wander in very wet or cold weather.

Green, oval-shaped eyes
These make an attractive contrast with the chocolate-brown coat.

Elegant yet muscular profile
This is reinforced by the relatively long, slender neck of these cats and their long legs.

Glossy coat
It should be a warm shade of chocolate-brown in color, possibly with a reddish-brown hue.

History

In the early days of cat showing, green-eyed, solid-colored, and blue-eyed pointed forms of the Siamese were shown. By the 1920s, the first group had fallen out of favor, and, since they could no longer be exhibited, such cats became extinct. In the early 1950s, however, a group of breeders in England decided that they wanted to try to recreate this type of cat and set up a breeding program for this purpose. Using a chocolate-point Siamese mated with a black shorthair, they produced a chestnut (chocolate) kitten. The breed was named after the Havana rabbit or a Havana ciger, thanks to its coloration. Unfortunately, however, since the large number of additions to the Oriental group, this founder member has now become scarce.

Character

The Havana Brown is a lively cat and uses its slim paws like hands on occasions, to turn over objects and hold down a piece of food that is too large to swallow in a single mouthful. Their appearance today tends to reflect the subsequent input of a Russian (see page 98) into their bloodline. This brought in the dilute gene, too, with blue the dilute form of black in terms of cat genetics. As a result, occasional lilacs (being the dilute form of chocolate) crop up in litters of Havana Browns as a legacy of such crossbreeding.

3. Japanese Bobtail

These very distinctive cats inspired the Japanese tradition of placing a ceramic ornament called Maneki Neko—translated as "Beckoning Cat"—in the windows of homes and businesses, where they are visible from outside. These ornaments are reputed to bring good fortune.

History

Cats were first imported to Japan from China more than 1,000 years ago, and at first were kept as pets of the nobility, frequently paraded walking on leashes. Then a plague of mice threatened to overrun the country, destroying everything, including all writings that were made on rice paper. This was at a time long before effective rodenticides, but luckily the cats triumphed, and they have enjoyed a special place in Japanese culture ever since. There are both longhaired and shorthaired forms of this breed, with the latter most common. Unlike the situation with the Manx (see page 132), Japanese Bobtails are never born without tails, or conversely, with full-length tails. Their bobtails are a universal feature.

FELINE CHARACTERISTICS		NOTES
Starting out	Still not common outside their homeland, especially in Europe.	
Personality	Very well-adjusted, friendly nature. Playful and affectionate.	Makes an ideal companion, especially for homes with children.
Appearance	Highly distinctive. Longhaired variant has a semi-longhaired coat.	
At home	Will settle very well, developing into a personable companion.	
Behavior	Not a good choice as a cat to live permanently indoors. Likes exploring.	Still retains hunting instincts, toward rodents especially.
Grooming	Needs to be more frequent when the coat is being shed. Not problematic, even in longhairs.	
Common health issues	Nothing significant reported. Watch for fleas if outdoors a lot.	No adverse health effects arising from the bobtail.

Triangular-shaped head
In the shape of an equilateral triangle, with the ears large and well spaced. Odd-eyed cats are favored.

Patterning

Any variety is accepted, aside from cats of colorpointed or Abyssinian type. Bicolors are common, with white predominating, and the calico (tortoiseshell-and-white, known as "mi-ki") form is traditionally favored. Japanese Bobtails are friendly cats, uttering a wide range of sounds. They enjoy chasing balls and can develop into very effective retrievers. In many ways, they are the ultimate house pets, getting along with dogs and children. They were unknown outside Japan until 1968, and although common in North America today, the breed remains scarce in Europe.

Pompom tail
This can be either straight or curled in some cases, but there are no effects on the spine elsewhere along the vertebral column.

Slender hind legs
These are longer than the front legs but generally kept bent so that the back appears level.

4. Mandalay

This is a breed native to New Zealand, developed in part from Burmese stock. It has built up a strong following in its homeland, not just for its sleek good looks but also for its charm and playfulness as a companion.

FELINE CHARACTERISTICS		NOTES
Starting out	Sleek, stylish companion, available in a range of colors.	
Personality	Demonstrative and extrovert, but also highly affectionate.	Thrives on attention, forming a close bond with people.
Appearance	Beautiful contrasting eyes complement the color of the coat.	
At home	Will appreciate plenty of opportunity to play and also climb.	Do not forget a scratching post, to keep the claws trim.
Behavior	Active, lively nature; wants to be fully involved in family life.	
Grooming	Smooth coat with little undercoat means minimal grooming required.	Combing and brushing does help improve the gloss on the coat.
Common health issues	No particular problems recorded.	

A colorful breed

The Bombay breed (see page 94) is very similar to the Mandalay, but whereas these cats are defined by their black coloration, the range of colors existing in the case of the Mandalay is significantly greater. Reds were prominent in the early stages of the breed's development, along with associated varieties including cream and tortoiseshell. Chocolate—of the same shade as the Havana Brown (see page 129)—plus lavender and blue forms are also popular now, along with cinnamons, fawns, apricots, and caramels, in addition to tabby and tortoiseshell variants.

History

The original breeding scheme that gave rise to these cats paired a Burmese (see page 56) with a nonpedigree cat. The impact has been partly to darken the Mandalay's appearance, compared with the Burmese, so that the ebony variety seen here is therefore black rather than brown, and the coloration is even, with no trace of points. The color of the eyes is deeper as well, varying from golden-yellow to amber, while the coat has a more luxurious, silky texture that requires relatively little grooming. The Mandalay came into being by accident, as the result of unplanned matings during the 1980s, between ordinary, nonpedigree cats and Burmese. Perhaps surprisingly, though, in spite of the attractive and intelligent nature of this breed, it remains essentially unknown elsewhere in the world.

Head shape
This should be in the form of an equilateral triangle, with the ears contributing to this impression.

Straight tail
This is of medium length, not thick at the base, and tapers little along its length, ending in a rounded tip.

Longer hind legs
These are slender and slightly taller than the front legs, with the paws oval in shape.

5. Manx

The Manx ranks among the best-known breeds of cats in the world, although it is far from common. These cats have a reputation for being highly intelligent and make excellent companions for people lucky enough to share their homes with them.

History

The precise origins of the Manx are shrouded in mystery, but what is certain is that it originates from the Isle of Man, located off England's west coast. It has been suggested that the ancestors of the breed are descended from cats that reached the island from a sinking Spanish galleon, after the Battle of the Armada in 1588. But it is more likely that the tail-less characteristic cropped up in the native cat population there as a result of natural inbreeding in a small population. The breed has a long history, being well represented at the early cat shows of the late 1800s. However, it is only tail-less individuals that can be shown.

FELINE CHARACTERISTICS		NOTES
Starting out	Affectionate, relatively large cat. Not widely available. Small litter sizes.	Not just a tail-less cat, as is popularly believed.
Personality	Friendly and will settle well in the home.	
Appearance	Very distinctive, with a square profile and a bunnylike gait.	This is a reflection of the fact that the front legs are shorter than the hind legs.
At home	Loyal but also appreciates the opportunity to wander outdoors.	
Behavior	Tolerant nature, getting along well not just with people but dogs.	
Grooming	Straightforward, although more frequent combing and brushing required.	
Common health issues	Kittens can suffer from spina bifida. Limb weakness and constipation can be issues, too.	Long-lived breed.

Attributes of the breed

Just as in the case of the Cymric (see page 69), Manx occur in three basic types. Those without tails are called rumpies, whereas stumpies possess long tails, and some Manx kittens have tails of almost normal length. Acceptable colors are basically those recognized for British Shorthairs, so that patterned forms, notably tabby and white variants, are quite common. Manx today have a rounded face and profile, whereas in the past, they were taller and thinner. They are highly adaptable and well-adjusted cats. There even used to be a well-known Manx that would accompany its Bulldog companion to dog shows in the 1920s, sharing its pen and seemingly enjoying the experience.

Good contrast
Clear delineation is important between the white and colored areas in the coat.

Square shape
The legs should be similar in length to those at the back, causing these cats to appear square in profile.

Long hind legs
The breed's hind legs are longer than the front legs, and the back is short, accounting for its distinctive gait, described as "bunny hopping."

6. Siamese

It is not just because of their svelte good looks that Siamese have become so popular. They rank as probably the most overtly affectionate breed and offer tremendous loyalty in return, being an ideal companion especially for someone living alone.

AT A GLANCE
- Very elegant
- Demonstrative nature
- Playful and agile
- Likes to climb

History

Early Siamese were very different from the breed seen today, with its angular shape. This appearance was developed increasingly after World War II. The range of colors also grew significantly at this stage, too, with new varieties such as cream points and red points being created, thanks to the introduction of the red gene to existing Siamese bloodlines. This was achieved very controversially by outcrossing to red-tabby Persian Longhairs during the 1930s. It was not until about 30 years later that Siamese finally gained acceptance for show purposes, albeit not always being described under this name, depending on the registration body. Some North American organizations recognize these lighter varieties separately as Colorpoint Shorthairs.

FELINE CHARACTERISTICS

For Feline Characteristics, see page 86

Angle of the eyes
The eyes slant down in the direction of the nose.

Elegant muzzle
The head is relatively long, as is the neck, with the large ears and alert eyes contributing to the breed's intelligent expression.

Suffusion on the flanks
This pale cream coloration will intensify as the cat becomes older, thanks to a fall in body temperature here.

Pale paws
The fur on the paws is paler than on the tail, with the patterning of tabby barring here being highly individual.

Colored tail
The cream coloration here is often more intense in these "new" colors than in the traditional colors of the Siamese.

What to expect

Just as in other cases, however, these cats are born white and then start to develop the color of their points from a few days of age. Tabby patterning is not uncommon, showing as a random pattern of distinctive barring on the legs. The eyes, as always in Siamese, must be the typical distinctive shade of blue. In terms of temperament, too, these new-colored cats are no different from other Siamese. They positively demand attention and are true extroverts, calling loudly if ignored in any way. Siamese will explore items with their front feet, so as to look underneath an object perhaps, or retrieve a ball that has gone under a chair during the course of a game, if they can reach it.

7. Turkish Angora

Many of the oldest cat breeds in the world originated in the vicinity of Turkey, with the Turkish Angora itself believed to have played a key role in the development of the Persian Longhair. It has become quite rare today.

History

The origins of the breed lie in the central part of Turkey, in the vicinity of Ankara, when this area was known as Angora. It is thought that they may represent a direct link back to the cats of ancient Egypt, having been resident in the vicinity of eastern Anatolia (Asia Minor) for more than a millennium, after being brought here by traders. The traditional color form of these cats is white, with odd-eyed individuals, having one blue and one amber eye, the most highly valued in their homeland. By the start of the last century, however, these cats had become so scarce in their homeland that a special breeding program to conserve them was started at Ankara Zoo, where it still continues today.

FELINE CHARACTERISTICS		NOTES
Starting out	Ancient bloodline, not to be confused with the modern Angora.	
Personality	Friendly and affectionate; used to living in the company of people.	
Appearance	A relatively short coat, plus a well-plumed tail.	White is the traditional color favored in the case of this breed.
At home	Makes a very affectionate companion; quite fastidious in terms of its coat care.	
Behavior	Curious and likes to explore but tends not to wander far.	
Grooming	Becomes more significant when shedding is occurring, in the spring especially.	Length of the coat varies significantly throughout the year.
Common health issues	Deafness is common in blue- or odd-eyed individuals.	Deafness in the case of odd-eyed whites afflicts the ear above the blue eye.

Narrow muzzle
The head is a modified wedge shape and relatively small in size. The eyes can be any color.

Long tail
This is covered with fur, especially during the winter months.

Silky coat
The coat has a fine texture, and there is no real undercoat, especially in the summer. The coat is longer and more impressive over the winter.

Tabby barrings
These markings are especially well defined on the legs, where the coat is short.

Color recognition

Although known across Europe for 500 years, Turkish Angoras were imported to the U.S. for the first time in 1963, obtaining full show recognition a decade later—but only for white cats of the breed, irrespective of their eye coloration. This situation continued until 1978, when other varieties, such as this brown tabby-and-white individual, were finally recognized for the first time. Turkish Angoras are now generally accepted in all colors and patterns, except for specific Oriental colors.

8. Turkish Van

This particular Turkish breed is localized to the area of Turkey around Lake Van, and remarkably, these cats sometimes go swimming in the lake, presumably to cool themselves. The breed was discovered by two English tourists who visited the area in 1955.

AT A GLANCE
- Incredible history
- Loves water
- Enjoys being groomed
- Distinctive patterning

FELINE CHARACTERISTICS		NOTES
Starting out	Not that common.	
Personality	Lively, curious, and affectionate.	
Appearance	White typically predominates in the coat, often with red-tabby areas.	Blue-eyed individuals tend not to suffer from deafness.
At home	Often fascinated by a dripping faucet; will sit and paw at the water droplets.	Not afraid to jump into a bath or even a pond outdoors, especially in hot weather.
Behavior	Likes being around people and has a playful side to its character.	
Grooming	This requires more time from the winter through to the spring.	Coat will be more profuse at this stage.
Common health issues	Hormonal problems and allergies affecting the skin have been reported.	

History

The tourists arranged to bring a pair of these cats to the U.K. The breed was slow to gain acceptance, and it was not until 1982 that they were first seen in the U.S. Their appearance has been shaped by their environment (hot in summer and very cold in winter). As a result, these cats grow a very thick coat in the winter, including a distinctive ruff. Then in the spring, this is shed, and with their single-layered coats, they do not look very dissimilar from ordinary shorthairs. The only part of the body where the hair remains long throughout the year is the tail.

Wide shoulders
This feature is quite distinctive, being affected by the breadth of the chest, and is especially evident in males.

Water-repellent coat
This means that after swimming, a cat dries off very quickly, while in the winter, rain and snow cannot cause chilling, even though there is no thick undercoat, as in most breeds.

Van pattern

The traditional red-and-white tabby patterning is seen here, but recently, it has emerged that pure white may be the preferred color of these cats in their homeland. Where there is a pattern, the color should be restricted to the head and tail, with a few random spots over the body being acceptable, too. An area of colored fur looking like a thumbprint on the left shoulder is typical. Eye color can be either blue or amber, or a combination, and in this case, blue-eyed individuals are not afflicted by congenital deafness. Occasional Turkish Vans with green eyes have been reported recently, but these are not favored by breeders.

Longer back legs
These are supported by powerful muscles that traditionally may have helped these cats swim.

9. Black and White

The tremendous variability that exists in the appearance of nonpedigree cats is part of their appeal, making each unique. They normally prove to be very friendly and adaptable companions, although they are individuals, with each tending to have its own particular quirks.

History

Nonpedigree cats have always had a reputation for resourcefulness. This is reflected by the way that they will often swap homes in order to gain food, giving the impression of being neglected, when in fact, they are simply in search of another meal! It is worth remembering that if a cat does become abandoned, it is likely to retain sufficient hunting skills in order to survive in the wild. This is why, in most major cities, there are populations of feral cats. These are individuals that are following a free-living existence, hunting and scavenging and avoiding contact with people as far as possible. Even young kittens born in such surroundings are almost impossible to tame, reflecting the fact that domestication in the case of the cat is not an irreversible process.

Appearance

Bicolored cats are common among the nonpedigree population, with self-colored (solid) individuals being rare, as they tend to be created by selective breeding. The markings in bicolors are highly random, though, with some predominantly colored, while others are mainly white. There generally does tend to be a white blaze between the eyes, though, broadening out over the jaws down onto the chest.

Alert expression
Facial shape tends to be rounded in most nonpedigrees, with the ears having slightly pointed tips.

Stout tail
Medium-length, this will taper along its length and usually ends in a rounded tip.

Intermingled fur
The contrast in the coat is less evident in nonpedigrees, and odd white hairs intermingled here in the black areas are common, compared with purebred cats.

Stocky build
Most nonpedigree cats tend to have quite thick and powerful legs. Their paws, too, are relatively large.

10. Classic Tabby and White

It is not just purebred cats that can have striking patterning, as shown by this individual. In fact, the classic tabby pattern associated with many breeds today arose in nonpedigrees of this type, before being introduced to pedigree bloodlines.

Keen nose
Scenting skills are important in cats, not just to find prey but also for communicating between themselves.

Mobile ears
These are quite flexible, and their position helps indicate the cat's mood.

Coat type
This short coat is quite weather resistant, ensuring that the cat will not become saturated when it rains, and it needs little grooming.

Tabby barring
The alternating light and dark rings extending down the tail are more variable in the case of nonpedigree tabbies, as in the case of the tabby markings on the body itself.

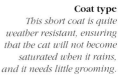

History

Ordinary domestic cats are curious by nature, and they can display a remarkable ability to memorize a clear picture of the area in which they live. Unneutered toms, in particular, can range over a wide area in the neighborhood. There are also hundreds of documented cases on record of nonpedigree cats being able to find their way home from some distance away, following a move. Studies have revealed that, initially, cats rely on the Earth's magnetic field to orientate themselves in the correct direction, but then, once back in familiar territory, they will follow recognizable landmarks to arrive at their previous homes. Kittens are less likely to have this ability, though, because they do not know the area well at this early stage in life.

Management

When you acquire a new cat, keep it indoors for at least two weeks, so as to reduce its desire to wander off. Having ready access to food and water, it will soon come to recognize your home as a safe refuge. You also need to teach your cat its name and encourage it to come to you when called. This will ultimately help ensure that you can call your cat back indoors easily at night or even during the day.

Cat types for people who have plenty of time available to care for their pets and will enjoy grooming them, as well as the bond that this will create.

Persian Longhair

High-maintenance Cats

Various breeds need differing amounts of care, depending largely on their coat type. Cats with long, dense coats will need grooming every day to prevent their fur from becoming matted. At the other extreme, the recent upsurge in interest in so-called "hairless breeds" has not been driven by low maintenance. Although it may appear that they need very little grooming, their care in this regard is actually potentially more demanding than that of even a longhaired cat.

Time spent on grooming is important in all cases, though, helping to reinforce the association between you and your cat. Just as significantly, it can also help ensure that your pet stays healthy. As you comb and brush the coat, you will be able to recognize signs of parasites such as fleas or even ticks, as well as possible abscesses or growths that will need veterinary treatment, not forgetting early warning signs of skin cancer, to which cats are not immune. The tips of the ears, especially of white cats, are especially vulnerable.

High-maintenance requirements may also extend into other aspects of your cat's life, especially if it is living inside as a house cat. You will need to set aside part of your home as an area where your cat can play. Equipment, too, such as a scratching post will be needed, to prevent your cat's claws from becoming overgrown and needing to be trimmed back with special clippers.

1. Don Sphynx

In spite of its name, this breed is quite separate from the Sphynx (see page 149). It has been known under a variety of different names, including the Don Hairless, the Russian Hairless, and the Donsky, as well as the Donskoy.

History

The Don Sphynx traces its origins back to 1987, with the discovery of a female hairless cat in the Russian town of Rostov-on-Don, which lies close to the northeast coast of the Black Sea. Christened Varya, she became the founder of the breed. Her first litter, produced in 1989, included both hairless and ordinary-coated kittens, which marked a significant difference with the Sphynx itself. This confirmed that the Don Sphynx was a completely separate mutation, with a dominant rather recessive mode of inheritance. This explained why hairless kittens resulted when Varya was mated to a cat with a normal coat. Initial recognition for the emerging breed was granted in 1997, and it has been possible to increase its numbers quite rapidly.

Appearance

Whereas the Sphynx has at least some fur apparent on the extremities of its body, the Don Sphynx is almost entirely hairless. Their color is derived entirely from that of their skin. Young kittens may be born with a light covering of hair in some cases, but this disappears as they grow older, so that by two years old, they are totally bald. Their bodies feel like velvet and are warm to the touch. As their build suggests, the Don Sphynx is also an athletic breed.

FELINE CHARACTERISTICS		NOTES
Starting out	Another Russian hairless breed that has recently been created.	Also known as the Donskoy.
Personality	Outgoing, friendly, and eager to be the center of attention in the home.	
Appearance	In spite of its hairless appearance, this is a new mutation from the Sphynx.	Has been developed using Oriental and Siamese outcrosses.
At home	Likes to play, and kittens especially are very energetic and athletic.	
Behavior	Lively nature means a play area indoors will be essential for these cats.	Not really suitable to be allowed outdoors.
Grooming	A damp cloth will be needed to wipe the cat's body. Check the ears, too.	
Common health issues	Do not wipe the coat over too frequently to remove excessive oil here.	This can trigger overproduction.

Fragile whiskers
They are present, being curly as in the case of a Rexed cat, but very fragile and easily broken off.

Long toes
These look more like fingers, due to the lack of a hair covering.

Long tail
This is very long and tapers conspicuously along its length.

2. Kinkalow

This short-legged breed is the result of combining two different spontaneous mutations that have arisen over recent years in the U.S. The Kinkalow has proved to be a friendly breed and is likely to attract growing attention.

History

Crossings between Munchkins (see page 82 and page 85) and American Curls (see page 105) are responsible for the development of these cats. Kinkalows have now been bred in a wide range of varieties, including self (solid) colors, as in this case, with glossy coats, through to lynx (tabby) and colorpointed individuals. There is also a longhaired form of the Kinkalow. Since this gene was present in both the founding breeds, so it was inevitable that it would emerge in Kinkalow bloodlines, too. The Kinkalow is with certainty the only breed of cat named after a copy store. Its founder, Terri Harris, was wondering what to call these cats and while visiting a FedEx Kinko's outlet, she was inspired, noting the breed's kinked ears and low legs.

Behavior

Kinkalows are attractive cats, and the shortcoated form needs little grooming. Nevertheless, it is not a good idea to allow them out, unless you have a secure backyard, simply because their short legs reduce their stride length. This makes it harder for a Kinkalow to outrun an aggressive cat in the neighborhood, and it may put them at a disadvantage in terms of crossing a road in the face of an approaching vehicle. There are no underlying medical problems inherited from the mutations underlying the breed's distinctive appearance.

FELINE CHARACTERISTICS

For Feline Characteristics, see page 81

Ear shape
The ears are turned slightly outward and rounded rather than pointed at their tips.

Color
Solid black coloration, with no hint of odd white hairs in the coat.

Size difference
In spite of the fact that this is a relatively small breed in terms of size, there is a distinction between the sexes, with males bigger than females.

Powerful paws
The legs are simply shortened, not weakened.

3. Lambkin

The Lambkin represents another of the new breeds being developed from the short-legged Munchkin (see page 82). Lambkins have a very distinctive appearance, in terms of their coat, combined with a friendly, lively nature, and they are being bred in a range of colors.

History

In this case, it has been the Selkirk Rex (see page 75) that has been combined with the Munchkin, to lay the foundation for the Lambkin, as these cats have become known. They were also described for a period as the Nanus Rex, with "nanus" meaning "small," but this name has not really caught on among breeders, compared with Lambkin. The roots of this name reside in the distinctive coat of these diminutive Rexes, which, especially in the case of white individuals, look not unlike that of a lamb. It has proved quite easy to create these cats, thanks to the nature of the genetic mutations involved, as both are the result of dominant genes. A Selkirk Rex paired with a Munchkin should result in a percentage of Lambkin kittens in each litter.

The future

At this stage, the Lambkin remains a scarce breed, but there is a good possibility that it will become established and continue to grow in popularity. This is firstly because of the relative ease with which these cats can be bred from their parent stock, and also as a reflection of their very attractive, cuddly look. Just like Selkirk Rexes, however, their coat will change in appearance between kittenhood and maturity. Both self-colored (solid) and patterned varieties exist.

FELINE CHARACTERISTICS		NOTES
Starting out	Another of the new dwarf breeds, and quite rare at present.	Bred from crossbreeding between Munchkins and Selkirk Rexes.
Personality	Bold and friendly nature; well adapted to family life. Quite placid.	
Appearance	Distinctive curly coat, available in a variety of colors and patterns.	Both longhaired and shorthaired forms exist, reflecting the Selkirk input into its origins.
At home	Can display a remarkable ability to climb rather than jumping up.	
Behavior	Affectionate and patient nature, making an excellent companion.	
Grooming	Quite straightforward, especially in the case of shorthaired cats.	
Common health issues	None recorded, with both the ancestral breeds being of nonpedigree origins.	

Coloration
A range of colors exist in the case of Lambkins, with this particular individual a dilute calico (tortoiseshell-and-white) individual.

Long tail
The length of the tail helps reinforce that of the body. It is relatively thick at the base.

Large eyes
These are rounded in shape and are a characteristic feature of this emerging breed.

Relatively long hind legs
The shortening of the limbs as a result of the Munchkin mutation is most apparent in the front legs.

4. LaPerm

The curly and wavy nature of the coat of these cats, with its distinctive Rexed appearance, helps explain why they are known as LaPerms. Active and extrovert by nature, the LaPerm is now being bred in many different colors and patterns.

Longhaired form
This is the longhaired form of the breed, as reflected by the length of the coat on the body and that on the tail.

Loose texture
The coat needs to have a loose, bouncy texture, not hugging the body, and a rather rough, unkempt appearance.

Tapering tail
The longest curls occur on this part of the body, as well as in the ruff and at the base of the ears.

History

The origins of all today's LaPerms can be traced back to a farm cat born in 1982, in a litter of kittens on a fruit farm in The Dalles, Oregon, owned by Linda and Richard Koehl. Christened Curly, she appeared rather bald at first, compared with the other kittens, but ultimately grew a curly coat with a soft texture. Later, Curly was nearly killed in an accident on the farm and so was kept indoors rather than being allowed to roam freely for a time, but she ended up pregnant.

Subsequent development

Ultimately, Curly gave birth to a litter of five male kittens, all of which displayed the same distinctive curly coat as herself. The number of such cats on the farm grew quite rapidly, as a result of this dominant mutation, and the curiosity of visitors persuaded Linda to discover more about them. She took some to a show, where they aroused considerable interest, and so the development of the breed began in earnest. There is no restriction on colors or patterning in the breed today, and Asian varieties such as chocolate are not uncommon, thanks to a random cross with a Siamese cat early in the LaPerm's development. Today, these Rexes are seen in many countries worldwide.

FELINE CHARACTERISTICS		NOTES
Starting out	Bred from farm stock, with longhaired and shorthaired forms recognized.	
Personality	Intelligent, straightforward, adaptable cats, that settle very well as pets.	
Appearance	Variable, from a tight curly coat through to a more wavy appearance.	Bred in a very wide range of colors, as well as patterned variants.
At home	Hardy breed that needs to be allowed outdoors regularly.	These cats may become difficult to manage if kept indoors for long periods.
Behavior	Retains hunting instincts, especially for rodents. Active cats by nature.	
Grooming	Coat type in this case is very variable. Shorthairs need far less coat care.	Kittens may be born without hair or become quite bald for a time.
Common health issues	A breed that has no serious health problems associated with it.	

5. Persian

The hairs in the coat of these cats are longer than those of any other breed. If they were placed end to end, they would stretch for around 230 miles (370 km)! Adequate time must be devoted to Persians every day for grooming purposes.

History

Owning a Persian is not something to be undertaken lightly, because without proper grooming, the long hair will soon start to mat, and it will be very difficult and distressing for your cat to try to remove these tangles by combing. It can often prove necessary to anesthetize a Persian with a neglected coat to cut back the worst areas, where the outer coat has merged with the dense woolly undercoat. The situation is especially problematic in the spring, when the dense winter coat is being shed, with the coats of these cats today being more profuse than they were back in the late 1800s when the breed was created. The range of colors and patterns is such that over 60 different varieties are recognized for show purposes today.

Face shape

Another change that has taken place is in the breed's facial profile. It has become more compact, to the extent that the most extreme examples are described as "Peke faces"—in reference to the Pekingese breed of dog with its very compressed face. Unfortunately, this has also interfered with the tear glands, the openings of which can be found just inside the lower lids, close to the nose. Tear fluid now often runs down the fur here, rather than draining away normally. These brownish deposits, often referred to as tear staining, will need to be wiped away regularly with moist cotton balls.

Widely spaced ears
They are small, low set, and located far back on the head. Long hair, described as furnishings, is present inside.

Well-furred tail
The tail is short, yet bushy in appearance, and proportionately matches the length of the body.

FELINE CHARACTERISTICS

For Feline Characteristics, see page 73

Long hair
This is at its most profuse on the body and tail, being significantly shorter on the face and the lower legs.

6. Longhaired American Curl

AT A GLANCE
- Unmistakable appearance
- Amenable disposition
- Grooming not difficult
- Ears can be vulnerable

The American Curl originally occurred in a longhair form, although such cats are now less common today, as shorthairs have become more popular. They are also more prevalent for genetic reasons as well, but the temperament of these cats is consistent.

History

Like many of the most distinctive characteristics introduced to domestic cat bloodlines over recent years, the American Curl is descended from a random mutation that was first noticed in a stray cat in 1981. Since then, this feature has not just led to the establishment of this breed, but it has been also successfully introduced to a number of others, as part of an ongoing process. In the case of longhaired American Curls, there are long tufts of fur protruding out of the ears, which are called furnishings. The ears themselves are much more open in such cats than normal, although it is impossible to distinguish which kittens in a litter will have curled ears at birth, as it will take several days for this feature to become apparent.

Grooming needs

The open nature of their ears does not disadvantage these cats, but they should be inspected every day, just in case any pieces of twig or other debris may have fallen down into the ear canal. Be very careful not to poke down there, especially with your fingers. A blunt-ended pair of tweezers will be a safer way to retrieve any items that have fallen down into the ear. The grooming of these cats in contrast is quite straightforward, as they do not have an especially dense coat.

FELINE CHARACTERISTICS

For Feline Characteristics, see page 105

Silky textured coat
This is soft and lies sleek and flat against the body, with little grooming required, even in the case of the longhaired variety.

Plumed tail
This has a profuse covering of fur, and in the case of bicolors, it generally consists of colored fur.

White coat
In the case of bicolors, this usually extends down on to the chest and underparts, but these cats can be bred in any color or pattern.

Medium-length legs
These appear straight when seen from the front or behind, with the feet in proportion and rounded in shape.

7. Longhaired Munchkin

The controversy in the cat world that greeted the arrival of the Munchkin (see page 82) as a spontaneous mutation back in 1981 has now largely abated, with these cats being increasingly widely kept today, and their soundness no longer being a significant issue.

(see page 82)

AT A GLANCE

- Unusual appearance
- Friendly nature
- Relatively easy to groom
- Intelligent nature

History

There was particular concern expressed with regards to longhaired Munchkins, compared with their shorthaired counterparts, because of fears that these cats would not be able to groom themselves. Although this has been proved not to be the case, longhaired Munchkins do need more grooming, as in the case of other breeds where both coat types exist, just to ensure that their plush coat does not become matted. While they are best kept as indoor cats, they are quite easy to train to walk on a harness and leash, so they can be exercised outdoors safely. Some owners have likened them to ferrets, partly because of their appearance, and they are certainly very active cats, usually eager to chase as part of a game. They are also very resourceful by nature.

Adaptability

Since Munchkins cannot leap up onto tables to steal food, they will try to find an alternative way, perhaps progressing via a chair to a kitchen table. The only evident change affecting their bodies is in terms of the length of their legs, and since they first started to be bred, Munchkins have been subjected to very extensive veterinary checks. These have not highlighted any significant specific medical problems associated with the breed, in either the short or longer term.

FELINE CHARACTERISTICS

For Feline Characteristics, see page 82

For Feline Characteristics, see page 82

Large ears
These are quite prominent and add to the impression of alertness that is a feature of these cats.

Gentle touch
The whisker pads are dark at their bases, highlighting their outline, while the whiskers themselves—which are sensory hairs—are relatively long and prominent.

Front legs
Shorter than the hind legs, these average about 3 in. (7.5 cm) in length.

Well-plumed tail
This is not shortened in any way, with the coat here being long.

Sitting upright
Munchkins often sit in this position, supporting themselves on their hind legs and looking around. This has led to them being nicknamed "kangaroo cats."

8. Peterbald

This is another recent addition to the world's cat breeds, which has been developed in Russia. They are quite variable cats, in terms of their appearance, and have proved to be excellent companions.

AT A GLANCE

• Variable degree of fur

• Coloration varies

• Oriental appearance

• Affectionate nature

FELINE CHARACTERISTICS		NOTES
Starting out	A relatively new development in the breeding of hairless cats.	
Personality	Curious, inquisitive, and will form a close bond with its owners.	
Appearance	Being developed on the svelte, elegant lines of a contemporary Oriental.	Long muzzle, widely spaced ears, with both a long neck and tail.
At home	Settles well but needs space. Its coat means the breed is best kept indoors.	Not noisy and will prove to be very loyal.
Behavior	Likes to explore around the home. Agile, too, so provide climbing facilities.	
Grooming	Coat type is variable—some are hairless, whereas others have a short coat.	Will be susceptible to cold as well as sunburn.
Common health issues	It is quite normal for kittens to lose their hair over time if not born with a full coat.	

History

This breed was created during 1984 in the city of St. Petersburg, Russia, having been bred from a mating between a Don Sphynx (see page 140) and an Oriental Shorthair. Four distinctive Peterbald cats were born, and have served as the breed's founders. The breed has since been developed quite quickly, first gaining show acceptance during 1996 in its homeland. The Peterbald was then awarded Provisional status in the U.S. during the following year and has since progressed to acquiring full Championship status in 2008. The type (appearance) of these cats has been modeled on that of Siamese and Oriental breeds, which have been extensively used as outcrosses for this purpose. This, in turn, has led to an increasing range of colors and patterns also becoming associated with the breed.

Appearance

An unusual characteristic of the Peterbald is the way in which it can have five distinctive coat types. These can range from ultra bald (as in the case of its Don Spyhnx ancestor) through flocked ("chamois") and velour to brush and even individuals that have a straight coat, recognizable by their normal, straight whiskers. Just like their ancestor, kittens (aside from those with full coats) can lose their coat as they start to mature. The care required depends to some extent on the type of the coat—for example, those without any coat will need to be protected, to guard against sunburn.

Brush form
This type of Peterbald has a thick, wiry covering of hair over its body. The whiskers are curly and may be kinked.

Oval paws
The paws are webbed and act like fingers, the Peterbald holding objects with them.

Long tail
Distinctive, whiplike shape adds to the breed's elegant appearance.

9. Skookum

The provisional name of this emerging breed has a range of meanings, but in this case, it simply translates as "really good," although it may be changed, because it can have negative connotations, too. However, there is no doubting the Skookum's affectionate nature.

Coloration
The color of the fur on the tail is not as intense, simply because it is longer and not as sleek when compared with that on the head, with the contrast being particularly apparent from this angle.

Prominent hairs
The whiskers and similar hairs above the eyes stand out in this particular breed, being very long.

Medium-length body
It has a slightly cobby appearance rather than long.

Expressive eyes
These are relatively large and help highlight the Skookum's appeal.

History

The development of the Skookum was pioneered by an American breeder named Roy Galusha, who crossed LaPerms (see page 143) with Munchkins (see page 82) intending to create a curly coated, short-legged breed as a result. Similar breeding programs have been carried out in other parts of the world, thanks to the relatively wide availability of both founder breeds. Both longhaired and shorthaired forms of the Skookum have resulted, mirroring the parent breeds. The coat is open-textured rather than dense, like that of the LaPerm, with the curls extending out and away from the body rather than lying close to it. These cats can be bred in any color or pattern, with colorpoint links tracing back to the early ancestry of the LaPerm.

Realities

Members of the Skookum will climb well and can jump quite effectively, too. They are intelligent cats. Males grow to a larger size than females. Grooming, as with the LaPerm, is needed about once a week, and it is a good idea to use a comb with revolving teeth, which will not flatten the curls. If a bath is required, allow the coat to dry naturally or use a towel. A hair-dryer (which upsets some cats) will cause it to become frizzy.

FELINE CHARACTERISTICS		NOTES
Starting out	A short-legged version of the La Perm, created with Munchkin input.	A relatively new breeding development and not numerous at present.
Personality	Easy going temperament derives from two breeds of nonpedigree origins.	
Appearance	Curled, wavy coat, creating ringlets, and can be shorthaired or longhaired in appearance.	Shorthaired form still has a coat with a springy texture.
At home	Makes a loyal, friendly companion, eager to be involved in family life.	Likes to venture out but watch for encounters with other cats.
Behavior	Alert and responsive, eager to play, and makes a good family pet.	
Grooming	Longhaired version of the breed needs more grooming than the shorthaired.	
Common health issues	None have been identified, and these have proved to be very healthy cats.	

10. Sphynx

This was the first of the hairless breeds to become established, back in 1966, and has since contributed to the development of several others. The Sphynx is best kept as an indoor companion, forming a close bond with those in its immediate circle.

AT A GLANCE

• Vulnerable to cold

• Does not like being held closely

• Sits alongside you

• Active, adaptable nature

FELINE CHARACTERISTICS		NOTES
Starting out	The original hairless breed that has now become more widely accepted.	Sometimes known as the Canadian Hairless, reflecting its origins.
Personality	A natural extrovert, as their appearance suggests. Very playful and affectionate.	
Appearance	Can occur in a wide range of patterns, creating a very distinctive appearance.	These cats feel warm to the touch, because of their relative lack of hair.
At home	Settles well in spacious surroundings indoors. At risk from sunburn outdoors.	
Behavior	Likes to curl up and sleep under a blanket to retain its body heat.	
Grooming	Wipe over the body every week to prevent the build-up of excessive oil.	In spite of its name, the body has a thin covering of hair, longer at its extremities.
Common health issues	May occasionally suffer from hypertrophic cardiomyopathy (HCM).	This is a degenerative heart condition.

History

Hairless mutations are not unusual in domestic animals, ranging from mice and guinea pigs to dogs. There were several reports of hairless cats before the Sphynx emerged in Canada. It was developed as a result of outcrossings to Devon Rex (see page 60) and is quite established today, having gained widespread publicity, for example, in the NBC comedy series *Friends*. Sphynx do usually have traces of longer hair, especially on the extremities of their bodies, and their coloration reflects the pigmentation in their skin. Those with pinkish-white coloration would be particularly at risk of sunburn if allowed outside, and Sphynx cats are also vulnerable to being injured in fights, because of their lack of fur. The skin may be wrinkled over some areas of the body, but overall, it tends to be quite sleek.

Care

It might be thought that because they only have a very short hair covering on their bodies, often described as "peach fuzz," the grooming care of the Sphynx would be minimal. In fact, they need to have a bath every week, using a damp sponge to remove natural body oil that accumulates on their skin. Their large, prominent ears may also need cleaning regularly with damp cotton balls, but do not use cotton swabs to probe down the ear canal, as this could cause serious injury. Instead, simply wipe the inside of the ear.

Bicolored markings
The black-and-white areas of the coat are evident in the skin and show up clearly on the face where the fur is longer.

Muscular body
The rump is distinctly rounded in shape, with males of this breed particularly muscled. The chest and abdomen are rounded, too.

Thick paw pads
These create an impression of cushions on the feet. The stopper pads higher up on the legs are also prominent.

Cat types for people who want something that stands out from the crowd, rather than an ordinary, nonpedigree or a purebred cat.

Brown Tabby

Torbie and White

Unique Cats

In many ways, these crosses can offer the best of both worlds, in terms of appearance and temperament, especially if you cannot make up your mind when choosing between two breeds. The downside is that such cats can be scarce, reflecting their origins. In many cases, they are simply the result of an unplanned mating that is unlikely to be repeated.

In a few cases, though, such pairings may have been carried out for a deliberate purpose, with the aim of creating a new breed. But it means that kittens surplus to the breeding program will be available, although again, the choice will probably be quite limited in terms of colors or patterns. You may also have to be patient, in terms of waiting for a kitten to become available.

Alternatively, it may be possible to acquire an adult cat that figured at an earlier stage in the breeding program. Breeders will sometimes sell cats under these circumstances, when they have more kittens becoming available, which are more in line with the type of cat that they are hoping to produce in their breeding programs. It is not a good idea to obtain a cat that has lived previously for all its life in a cattery rather than in the home, because it may not settle as readily in these surroundings and is likely to be shy.

Red Tabby and White

1. Siberian Crossbreed

Cats with long coats are less common in the general cat population than their shortcoated counterparts, partly because this characteristic is recessive in genetic terms. Yet they can be strikingly attractive, even if they are not brightly colored.

AT A GLANCE

- Long coat
- Typically bicolor
- Relatively quiet
- An outdoor cat

History

The dense coat of the Siberian (see page 76) evolved naturally, to give protection against the bitter cold in its homeland, rather than being created for exhibition purposes. These cats represent what is effectively a natural longhaired population of ordinary domestic cats that have bred over the course of centuries, evolving a distinctive appearance shaped by their environment. Only quite recently, since the start of the Glasnost era in the 1980s, has the breed reached the West. Being active, outdoor cats, Siberians need space in which to be able to roam, and this can sometimes lead to unexpected litters.

Appearance

This particular cat has a much longer, more profuse coat than that of a typical nonpedigree, reflecting the Siberian input into its ancestry. During the summer, the coat will become significantly shorter and the ruff of longer fur under the chin will be lost. The coloration here is typical of an ordinary domestic cat, with random black-and-white markings. The striking green color of the eyes is particularly attractive. Regular grooming will be essential with cats of this type, especially when they are shedding their winter coats. Otherwise, there is a real risk that they will develop fur balls in the stomach, by swallowing loose fur as they groom themselves, which then forms a mat here.

Prominent whiskers
These help the cat judge whether it can slip through narrow openings, without becoming stuck.

No distinct patterning
The black-and-white areas in the coat are variable, and littermates will all be individually marked.

Relatively large
The Siberian input has ensured that this individual is bigger in size than a typical nonpedigree longhair.

2. British Shorthair and Persian

This is one of the better-known interbreed pairings, which ultimately led to the creation of the Exotic Shorthair (see page 47). The cat pictured here is a first generation mating and displays attributes of both breeds in its appearance and temperament.

AT A GLANCE

- Cuddly appearance
- Large eyes
- Quiet nature
- Stocky build

Tortoiseshell coloration
This is an unusual lilac tortoiseshell-and-white cat, with lilac coloration in British Shorthairs stemming from longhaired pairings. Cream coloration is evident between the eyes.

Large eyes
These are a feature of both breeds, being rounded and orangey in color in this case.

History

Crosses between the emerging British Shorthair breed (see page 46) and Persian (see page 144) have taken place intermittently since the earliest days of cat showing. The original purpose was to introduce greater size to the emerging shorthaired breed, which had been created from ordinary street cats. Having achieved this, the cats were then bred in such a way as to eliminate the longhaired gene from the bloodline, and the classic coat type of the British Shorthair was restored. More recently however, it has also proved possible to introduce new colors to the breed by this means, since with more than 60 recognized colors and patterns within the Persian group, these cats offer considerable potential for this purpose.

The result

Cats bred from such pairings are relatively large, but their heads are not generally as wide as in the case of a Persian. The flattened facial shape of this breed has also been affected, so the nasal area is not as compressed, but males will develop the characteristic swollen area, called jowls, on their cheeks when they mature. Nevertheless, there will be individual differences between littermates, with some tending to resemble Persians more closely than British Shorthairs and vice versa. There is no standardization when two different breeds are crossed in this way.

Coloration
As in patterned pedigree cats generally, the individual colors are still well defined in this case.

Symmetrical markings
Both the front legs are white, as is the area from the chin down onto the chest, but such markings are individual in crossbred cats.

3. British Shorthair Cross

Not all nonpedigree pairings result in cats that are significantly different from the breed itself. It is also unlikely that the temperament of the cat will be altered significantly over the course of one generation—certainly not in this case.

AT A GLANCE

- Individual appearance
- Strong British Shorthair influence
- Affectionate nature
- Easy-care coat

History

The British Shorthair is actually a breed created directly from ordinary cats that were to be found on the streets of Victorian Great Britain back in the 1800s. Today, although such cats are significantly larger in size, with a cobby appearance, they still retain a basic link back to this original gene pool. This characteristic, perhaps more than anything else, is reflected in their temperament, with these shorthairs being closer to ordinary nondomestic cats in this respect than most other breeds, aside from their American and European counterparts. They are friendly yet not unduly demonstrative, and they are moderately vocal, too. Combining British Shorthairs with nonpedigree cats will therefore not radically transform the personalities of their kittens, either.

Nonpedigree matings

It is also possible for recognized pedigree cats to mate with others of their kind, for which pedigree papers are not available. Not all breeders are eager to pass on this information to new owners simply seeking one of their kittens as a pet, partly as a means of deterring them from breeding with their cat in due course. This is because it is likely not to be of the best show quality, having minor flaws such as imperfections in color, for example. Such cats will still make excellent companions, however, and will be significantly less expensive than acquiring a potential prize-winning individual. In fact, without an experienced eye, it is quite likely that you will be unable to spot why a particular kitten would not excel as a show cat.

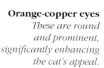

Orange-copper eyes
These are round and prominent, significantly enhancing the cat's appeal.

Blue-cream coloration
This cat is a dilute tortoiseshell, although its patterning is very poor, compared with the judging standard for the blue-cream variety.

Powerful legs
These are straight and well boned, like those of a pedigree British Shorthair.

4. Red-and-white Mixed Breed

The origins of many nonpedigree cats are not clear, with the characteristic signs of any breed that may have been involved in their development having effectively become diluted as the result of further, more recent nonpedigree pairings.

History

Tabby-and-white areas on the coat always tend to be indicative of nonpedigree roots, but other features may be suggestive of some purebred input in the past. This may relate to the appearance of the coat or its texture or the proportions of the body. A lot also depends on the stability of the cat population in question. Many of today's popular breeds have started from restricted gene pools, which, in turn, have then shaped the cat's appearance. Such breeds are sometimes described as being "natural" as a result, meaning that they were free from the interference of people during their early stages of development. The appearance of such cats may be influenced by the climate, as in the Norwegian Forest Cat (see page 72).

Appearance of the coat

In most cases, the influence of the longhaired gene is never as pronounced in nonpedigree as it is in pedigree bloodlines. In many cases, longhaired nonpedigrees can only be recognized, especially during the summer months, by a plumed tail displaying much longer hair than is apparent on the body. They may also show a ruff of longer hair on the chest, particularly during the winter, when the weather tends to be colder, with the remainder of their coat relatively short and smooth.

Less profuse coat
The coat on the body is short, which helps highlight the tabby patterning evident here.

Neck shape
The longer hair on the neck can appear to make the cat's head look relatively small.

Mixed colors
The way in which the colored and white areas are arranged in the coat is entirely random, being an individual feature.

5. Black and White

Although there may be no obvious sign of a purebred past in a cat's appearance, there may be an indication from its size. This reflects the fact that nonpedigree cats of this color are often smaller than their purebred counterparts.

History

Black-and-white coloration, like that of other bicolors, has proved to be a very difficult trait to stabilize. During the early days of the British Shorthairs, these particular cats, known as magpies after the bird in the case of the black-and-white variety, became very rare as a result. Breeders lost interest because it was too difficult to create cats with an ideal patterning, based on the show standard. The original aim was to breed them with similar patterning to Dutch rabbits, which are also bicolored, displaying a white area around the middle of their bodies. This had to be changed because it was not feasible to develop and standardize similar patterning. Even today, bicolored kittens, even in the same litter, can have a remarkably different appearance.

Overall appearance

This bicolor patterning can also be apparent on other parts of the body. In this case, there is an area of black pigment clearly evident on the nose, being highlighted here because the surrounding fur is white, although black pigment could have extended into this area as well. If you look at the paw pads of black-and-white cats, it is not uncommon to find similar patches of black here, set against pink areas, which correspond to areas of white fur in the coat. Each cat of this type will have a highly individual appearance—more so than in the case of their purebred counterparts. In cases where white fur predominates overall, with restricted black areas evident mainly on the head, such cats are sometimes described as having "Van" patterning, after that associated with the Turkish Van breed (see page 135).

Color mix
It is not unusual for white hairs to be evident in black areas of the coat in the case of nonpedigree cats.

Medium-length tail
This is relatively thick, and does not taper significantly along its length.

Tail coloration
In some bicolors of this type, the tail is white.

6. Blue-and-white Burmese Cross

It is frequently not possible to tell the sire of a litter of kittens with any certainty when mating occurs randomly. This could only be confirmed by the use of DNA technology, although the appearance of the kittens can give clues.

History

Cats of all true domestic breeds can interbreed freely with each other, as they share the same ancestor, in the guise of the African Wild Cat (*Felis silvestris lybica*). They therefore all have the same number of chromosomes, and their offspring will be fully fertile, as far as genetic compatibility is concerned. If there are genetic problems, these will be linked to the mutation itself, although they are uncommon. The best-known example involves the Manx (see page 132), tail-less examples of which must not be paired with each other, but to cats with normal tails that crop up in Manx litters as well. Only in the case of very recent wild cat crosses may fertilization create difficulties, with the early males tending to be infertile.

This case

Trying to unravel the ancestry of a crossbred cat from its appearance is not a precise science, but both physical features and coloration can be significant. In this case, the cat is bigger than its Burmese ancestor, with long front legs. The white patterning on the paws is strongly reminiscent of a Snowshoe (see page 99), whereas both its posture, arising in part from its relatively long front legs, and coloration is more akin to that of a Russian (see page 98).

Long neck
This increases the appearance of the cat's height, adding to its body length.

Blue coloration
The actual depth of color can vary, being a grayish shade. Here it is broken with white.

AT A GLANCE

- One-off
- DNA needed for ancestral proof
- Easily groomed coat
- Quite loud and affectionate

Long, straight front legs
These are similar to those of a Russian, giving a clue to the breed's ancestry. The toes are rounded in appearance.

7. Siamese Crossbreed

Cats with Siamese patterning have long been popular as pets, although it is not just their patterning but their contrasting blue eyes that appeal to many owners. This feature is often retained in cases where Siamese have mated with other breeds, too.

AT A GLANCE
- More rounded appearance
- Heavier build
- Darker body color
- Less distinctive point color

History

Given the popularity of Siamese (see page 86), it is perhaps not surprising that attempts have been made to superimpose their distinctive appearance onto other breeds. This began back in the 1920s with the Himalayan, which is essentially the colorpoint counterpart of the Persian Longhair. More recently, breeders have sought to develop a colorpoint form of the British Shorthair, with considerable success, by the use of Siamese crosses. The general impact of any crossbreeding with contemporary Siamese is to lose their distinctive angular facial shape, though, resulting in cats that are more akin to the traditional form of the breed, sometimes known as the Applehead. These particular Siamese cats are now becoming more popular again in their own right.

Personality

The temperament of Siamese crosses will be more moderate than that of pure Siamese. They will be quieter and will also be less inclined to climb, either in the home or outside. These cats will still be highly affectionate, however, and form a strong bond with their owners. Their grooming needs, at least in the case of shorthaired crosses, will be fairly minimal, although they are likely to display more of an undercoat than true Siamese, where the sleek outline of such cats is reinforced by the relative absence of this feature.

Mackerel tabby
The influence of the outcross is clearly evident here in this cat's coat, with mackerel tabby patterning evident on the sides of the body.

Rounded eyes
This is not a characteristic associated with Siamese themselves, whose eyes are more angular in appearance.

Points maintained
These are not evenly colored, as in Siamese. Instead, the tail is considerably darker than the feet.

8. Siamese Crossbreed

The darker areas on the extremities of the body, constituting the points, are maintained in this particular Siamese cross, but its eye color has been modified from that of the Siamese itself. The shape of the ears is also different.

AT A GLANCE
- Relatively stout body
- Tabby markings
- Long neck
- Points apparent

History

The precocious nature of the Siamese is often responsible for unexpected litters of kittens, because these cats can be sexually mature when only three months old. A female Siamese let out at this age may then end up mating with one or more typically nonpedigree cats in the neighborhood, producing kittens that are then likely to grow to a larger size than she is herself. As with true Siamese, they are likely to be white at birth and will then start to develop their highly individual appearance within a few days. The shading on the body will continue to become more pronounced as the cat grows older, which is another feature seen in Siamese.

Impact

Such crosses may lack both the elegance of the Siamese itself, as well as the attractive patterning associated with this breed. This is almost certainly the case where, although the cat is unique in terms of its looks, it is not so instantly appealing in terms of appearance as its parents. It reflects the difficulties that breeders can face when seeking to establish new breeds, as not all kittens will necessarily prove to combine the desired features of their parents. Here, the coat has become rougher, rather than lying sleek. Where a particularly desirable feature has been diluted or even disappeared in an evolving breed, it becomes important to mate such cats back to that breed, in order to re-emphasize it again in the future, so it does not become lost. Standardizing the cat's type (appearance), which is what creating a breed involves, proves to be very much a matter of checks and balances. Constant refinement is required in the early days, by selecting only the most suitable cats for breeding purposes.

Tabby patterning
Very distinct tabby lines are evident on the head of this individual, suggesting the likely identity of its nonpedigree parent.

Long neck
This is thicker than in the case of true Siamese, with the head quite small.

Body coloration
The cat's appearance will darken with age, as is typical of individuals displaying colorpointed patterning.

Dark stripes
The tabby barring is very evident here on the legs, with the feet coarser than those of Siamese.

9. Siamese and Chartreux

This very rare interbred cross has resulted in an imposing cat that bears relatively little direct resemblance to either of the parent breeds. There is no way of predicting just how such kittens will appear until after they are born.

History

There is no guarantee that a Siamese crossbreed will display a consistent point color, as shown by this case. In some respects, this individual is rather reminiscent of a bicolored Ragdoll (see page 32), although it is obviously a shortcoated cat. There have been several cases, such as the Burmilla (see page 48), where the appearance of the offspring resulting from an unplanned mating between two existing breeds have served as inspiration to develop a new breed. This can only be achieved over a number of generations, though, both to fix the type (appearance) of the cat and also to establish its pattern of markings. It requires outcrossings back to the founder breeds, as well as a very clear idea of what the desired end result is, in terms of the emerging breed's characteristics. However, the likelihood is that, if kittens with a particular patterning crop up in a litter, then it is possible that others with similar patterning may result in subsequent litters. This then opens the way to develop a breeding program that will "fix" these traits over subsequent generations.

Temperament

It is not just physical features that are likely to merge in the resulting kittens, but also behavioral aspects of the breeds, too. In this case, such cats will almost certainly prove to be sharp hunters. The ancestors of the Chartreux (see page 107) reputedly came from the mountains of Syria, where they lived by hunting, and certainly, this trait remains strong in the breed today. The modern Siamese, for its part, is also very adept when it comes to hunting, due in part to its natural athleticism. These cats will climb trees and may even catch unwary birds among the branches.

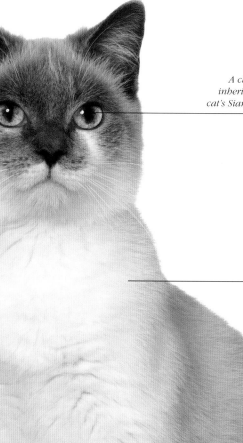

Blue eyes
A characteristic inherited from the cat's Siamese parent.

Woolly coat
This texture reflects the Chartreux's input into the cat's ancestry.

Bicolor body
Light coloration here is offset against white coloration, with the tail much darker.

10. Angora and European Shorthair

The more extreme, angular, Oriental appearance of the Angora breed has been rounded off, due to the input of European Shorthair blood into this cat's ancestry. The distinctive green coloration of the eyes is, however, a characteristic feature inherited from the Angora (see page 57).

History

This is a fairly localized cross, as European Shorthairs (see page 108) are rarely encountered outside mainland Europe, but the likelihood is that cats with a similar appearance might result from the use of American Shorthairs (see page 104) instead. The similarity between these shorthaired breeds and nonpedigree cats also suggests that crossbred Angoras produced from domestic cats might be similar as well, but would probably be smaller in size. The coat length of such individuals is likely to vary significantly through the year, since Angoras shed much of their long hair in the spring, so that they resemble shorthaired cats during the summer months, aside from a long plume of fur on the tail at this stage. The coat will then regrow during the following fall.

Appearance

The colors that can arise in such cats depend on their parents. Both Angoras and European Shorthairs occur in a wide range of colors and patterns, but tabby markings in crosses of this type will be fairly indistinct, certainly when compared with European Shorthair tabby forms. This is a reflection of the length of the coat, and the fact that it is not sleek, thereby ensuring that the markings in the fur are less intense as a result.

Short hair
The fur on the back of the ears is soft and velvety, whereas there is longer fur, described as furnishings, within the ears themselves.

AT A GLANCE

- Long variable coat
- Range of colors
- Stunning eyes
- Affectionate nature

Ruff of fur
There is a long ruff of fur present on the chest here, which will be far less conspicuous during the summer.

White lips
The white area around the jaws is likely to be a feature inherited from this cat's European Shorthair parent.

Caring for Cats

Taking care of cats has never been easier—and this is part of the reason underlying their popularity as pets. No longer is there a need to cook food specially for them, with the associated difficulty of ensuring that they have a balanced diet. Instead, there is a wide range of specially prepared foods to choose from, which are easily obtained from a variety of outlets.

Feeding considerations

A greatly improved understanding of the nutritional needs of cats helps explain why they are now living much longer than in the past. Kittens born today have a life expectancy that is likely to extend into their mid-teens or beyond. Lifestage diets are valuable in catering for their needs at different stages in their lives. There are such foods available for kittens, adults, and senior cats, produced by various pet food manufacturers.

However, the brand of food that you choose may not be very significant, as they are all formulated to meet specific nutritional guidelines, thereby ensuring that your pet receives all the nutrients that are required. In fact, there is often no need to purchase premium brands, although if your cat does turn out to be a fussy eater, then this may be necessary.

Cats can often prove to be quite fickle about food, eating one flavor or brand readily but then losing interest in it. If this happens, there is no need to dispose of the unopened cans or pouches. Simply wait for a couple of months—assuming the food will still be in date— and then reintroduce it to your cat's diet. You should then find that your pet once again eats this food readily.

The major difference in terms of choice is between so-called "dry" and "wet" food, which has a significantly higher water content. Dry food offers a much more concentrated source of energy, and so cats need proportionately less, in comparison with wet food. Stick carefully to the recommended on-pack feeding instructions, because if you overfeed your cat on a regular basis, the likelihood is that it will soon become overweight.

Obesity will endanger its health, triggering weight-related illnesses, such as *diabetes mellitus*, potentially shortening its life as a result. Although it is possible to slim down an overweight cat, this can be difficult, as your pet may simply start to wander next door to get food there or elsewhere in the neighborhood.

Drinking

Once open, packs of dry food can be stored without the need to refrigerate them. Cats fed on dry food will tend to drink more, but in any case, your pet should always have a clean bowl of water available. There is absolutely no need to offer milk to your cat, especially as, in many cases, this will simply cause a digestive upset.

Many cats, especially Oriental breeds such as the Siamese, lack the necessary enzyme to break down the milk sugar component, known as lactose, which is then likely to ferment in the intestinal tract. If you do want to provide something other than water, there are specially formulated lactose-free milks produced for cats.

Store-bought cat food contains all the nutrients your cat needs— although some pet owners choose to make their own cat food.

*Nonpedigree Tabby
Longhair*

Grooming

A cat's grooming requirements depend very much on the individual. As a general guide, longhaired cats will need daily grooming. Special grooming combs will be useful to prevent tangling, and ultimately, matting of the fur.

It helps to choose a design that has revolving teeth. These will pass through the fur more easily, being less likely to pull at the hair, which will otherwise prove to be distressing for your pet. Beware when using grooming brushes for this reason, although they can be very useful, especially for removing loose hair from the coat when your cat is shedding.

What you do not want is to upset your cat so that it comes to resent being groomed. This can create great difficulties. It is therefore very important to start grooming cats while they are still kittens, as they tend to be more tolerant at this stage and are less likely to rebel against being groomed as they grow older. The coats of longhaired kittens are also not as profuse at this stage, compared with adults of the same breed, which helps, in terms of accustoming them to this experience.

HEALTH ISSUES

Most cats rarely get sick, but problems can crop up occasionally, and some of the warning signs of a potential health issue are as follows:

- Ongoing loss of interest in food.
- A discharge from the eyes and/or nostrils, with coughing and sneezing.
- Emergence of the "third eyelid," or haws—a membrane that appears at the the corner of the eyes.
- Any unexplained swelling over the body.
- Dribbling—typically indicative of a dental problem.
- Limping—can be linked to an accident or may indicate a circulatory problem.
- Any significant behavioral change, such as sleeping longer than normal.
- Soiling indoors, away from the litter tray, especially if there is diarrhea.
- Persistent scratching and hair loss.

Cleanliness

Cleanliness is very important when feeding cats, and not just for health reasons. They can be very fussy if fed from a dirty bowl, refusing the food. Always wash your cat's bowl after each meal and change the drinking water every day. Equally, if your cat is using a litter tray, be sure to keep this clean, because otherwise, your pet may choose to relieve itself elsewhere in the home.

Dilute Tortoiseshell Shorthair

The Human Selector

What you need to consider

After deciding that you can and want to make the commitment to have a cat, the next question that arises is what sort of domestic cat would be most appropriate for your lifestyle? Although cats generally display far less range in size than dogs, they nevertheless do differ significantly, both in terms of temperament and the care that they require. The charts below are intended to act as a guide, to help you identify your ideal feline companion.

Red European Burmese

Is this the first time you've owned a cat?

NO, I'VE ALWAYS HAD A CAT	I HAD A CAT WHEN I WAS YOUNGER	I'VE NEVER HAD A CAT
In theory, there is no reason as to why you could not have any breed, depending on your other responses to the questions below.	You could consider most breeds, but the Exotic Shorthair, Ocicat, and Scottish Fold could be of particular interest.	Probably best to stick with one of the more placid varieties, such as the American or British Shorthairs, the Abyssinian, or the Ragdoll.

Do you have any other pets?

NO, AND I ONLY WANT ONE	I HAVE ANOTHER CAT	I HAVE VARIOUS PETS
See the Siamese, Bengal, Oriental, and Somali entries.	Some, such as the Burmilla, Chartreux, and Persian, are more social than others.	Those that are likely to be unfazed include the Persian and Himalayan (Colorpoint Longhairs), plus the Turkish Van.

Do you have a yard?

YES, AWAY FROM ROADS	A SMALL URBAN YARD	NO, I DON'T
Breeds such as the Maine Coon, Norwegian Forest Cat, and the Siberian Cat are possibilities.	Your choice might range from the unusual Munchkin to the ordinary domestic cat.	Consider breeds such as the Devon Rex and Sphynx, and even the Burmese.

Do you live on your own?

YES, I'M ON MY OWN	NO, THERE ARE TWO OF US	NO, WE HAVE CHILDREN, TOO
Both the Korat and Russian Shorthair, plus the Angora breeds, could be among your choices.	You may want to consider the American Curl, Bengal, or Birman breeds.	The Selkirk Rex, Spotted Mist, and the European Shorthair, if you have older children, could be suitable.

NOW COUNT 5 POINTS FOR EVERY LEFT-HAND ANSWER,
3 POINTS FOR EVERY MIDDLE ANSWER, AND 1 POINT FOR EVERY RIGHT-HAND ANSWER

15 or over: A wide range of cat breeds will suit you, and your living accommodation will accommodate most of them.

10 or over: There is a perfect cat for you, but you will have to be more careful selecting a breed that suits your specific needs.

Less than 5: You will need to think very carefully about having a cat. Although some cats will suit you better than others, all cats needs both attention and suitable living surroundings. A cat should not be brought into an environment that is too restricted by your busy lifestyle.

Before you make your final choice, you need to consider your own personality, too, to ensure that you can bond well with your chosen cat.

Are you seeking a soulmate as a companion?

Are you especially interested in Eastern mythology, as the ancestors of many cat breeds can be traced back to this part of the world, and their personalities are quite different from those which have been bred in the West?

Do you have a fair amount of free time on your hands? In which case, you can choose a longhaired breed whose care may require considerable grooming.

On the other hand, if you are busy, then opting for its shortcoated counterpart is likely to be a better option.

Using the chart below should help you gain further insight into making the correct choice.

THINGS THAT I HAVE

Money	On a tight budget? Consider acquiring an ordinary domestic cat.	With some money? Consider a British or American Shorthair.	With money to spare? See the Bengal or Californian Spangled.
Time	Time is tight? Consider a Cornish Rex or Exotic Shorthair.	With more free time? Think about a Balinese or Snowshoe.	Plenty of time? A Persian or Ragamuffin may be suitable.
Space	Bijou living? Consider a Sphynx or Peterbald.	More space? See Bombay or Tonkinese.	Plenty of space? A Maine Coon or Pixiebob may be suitable.
Athleticism	Prefer to spend time on the sofa? See Persian or Himalayan.	Enjoy being active? See Egyptian Mau, Manx, Singapura, or Nebelung.	A breed with a lively nature? See Siamese, Oriental, or Maine Coon.

THINGS THAT I WANT IN MY CAT

A clever cat	Fun and cute? See Persian or Himalayan Longhair.	More intelligent? See Exotic, Burmese, or Birman.	Most intelligent? See Manx, British Shorthair, or Siamese.
A friendly lap cat	More independent? See Norwegian Forest Cat or Siberian.	Loyal companion? See Exotic Shorthair or Oriental.	One that spends most time with you? See Ragdoll or Abyssinian.
A cat that needs little grooming	More grooming? See Himalayan (Colorpoint Longhair) or Persian.	Medium grooming needs? Consider Cymric, Kurilian Bobtail, and Balinese.	Easy-care coat? See Singapura, Bombay, and Sokoke.
A quiet cat	Noisy natures? See the Siamese and Korat.	Moderately vocal? Consider the Russian Shorthair or Somali.	Quietest? Consider the Persian. Exotic Shorthairs are also not very vocal.
A loyal cat	Most independent? Maine Coon or Pixiebob.	Decidedly friendly? British Shorthair, Siamese, or Scottish Fold.	Most loyal? Abyssinian, Ragdoll, and Birman.

The Cat Selector

The following chart provides some insights into choosing a particular cat, although a number of factors can influence the suitability of a particular individual. Kittens in general will settle more readily without problems, compared with older cats whose background may have resulted in them becoming instinctively nervous. Under each category in the chart below, certain types of cats are highlighted with a special star (✪) as being potentially the most suitable for specific situations, depending on your living arrangements.

THE CAT SELECTOR

BREED	Active nature	Grooming needs	Suitable for older owners	Suitable for families
Abyssinian	★★★	★	★★★	✪
American Bobtail	★★★	★★	★★	★★★
American Curl (longhaired)	★★★	★★★	★★	★
American Curl (shorthaired)	★★★	★	★★	★
American Ringtail	★★	★★	★★★	★★
American Shorthair	★★	★	★★	★★★
American Wirehair	★★★	★★	★★★	★★
Angora	★★★	★★	★★★	★★
Ashera	★★★	★	★	★★
Australian Mist	★★	★	✪	✪
Balinese	★★★	★★	★★	★★
Bambino Dwarf	★★	★★	★★	★
Bengal	★★★	★	★★	★★
Birman	★★	★★★	★★★	★★
Bombay	★★★	★	★★★	★★★
British Shorthair	★★★	★	✪	✪
Burmese	★★★	★	✪	★★★
Burmilla	★★	★★	✪	✪
Californian Spangled	★★★	★	★★★	★★★
Chartreux	★★★	★	★★	★★
Chausie	★★★	★	★	★
Cornish Rex	★★★	★	★★	★★

BREED	Active nature	Grooming needs	Suitable for older owners	Suitable for families
Cymric	★★★	★★★	★	★★
Devon Rex	★★★	★★	★★★	★★
Don Sphynx	★★	★★	★★	★
Egyptian Mau	★★★	★	★★	★★
Elf	★★	★★	★★	★★
European Burmese	★★★	★	★★★	★★★
European Shorthair	★★★	★	★★★	★★★
Exotic Shorthair	★★	★★	★★	★★
German Rex	★★★	★★	★★★	★★
Havana Brown	★★★	★	★★★	★★
Himalayan (Colorpoint Longhair)	★	★★★	★★★	★★
Japanese Bobtail	★★★	★	★★	★★★
Kinkalow (longhaired)	★★	★★★	★★	★★
Kinkalow (shorthaired)	★★	★	★★	★★★
Korat	★★★	★	★★	★★
Kurelian Bobtail	★★★	★★	★	★★
Lambkin	★★	★★★	★★	★★
LaPerm	★★★	★★★	★★	★★★
Maine Coon	★★★	★	★★	★★★
Mandalay	★★★	★	★★★	★★★
Manx	★★★	★	★★	★★★
MinPer	★	★★★	★★★	★★
Munchkin (longhaired)	★★★	★★	★★	★★

Tabby Maine Coon

BREED	Active nature	Grooming needs	Suitable for older owners	Suitable for families
Munchkin (shorthaired)	★★★	★	★★	★★
Napoleon	★★	★★★	★★★	★
Nebelung	★★★	★★★	★★★	★★
Norwegian Forest Cat	★★★	★★★	★★	★★★
Ocicat	★★★	★	★★★	✪
Ojos Azules	★★★	★	★★	★★
Persian	★	★★★	★★★	★★
Peterbald	★★★	★★	★★	★★
Pixiebob	★★★	★★	★★	★★★
Ragamuffin	★★	★★★	✪	✪
Ragdoll	★★	★★★	✪	✪
Russian	★★★	★	★★	★★
Safari	★★★	★	★	★
Savannah	★★★	★	★	★
Scottish Fold (longhaired)	★★★	★★★	★★	★★
Scottish Fold (shorthaired)	★★★	★	★★★	★★★
Selkirk Rex (longhaired)	★★★	★★★	★★	★★
Selkirk Rex (shorthaired)	★★★	★★	★★★	★★★
Serengeti	★★★	★	★	★
Siamese	★★★	★	★★★	★★
Siberian	★★★	★★★	★	★★★
Singapura	★★★	★	★★	★★★
Skookum	★★	★★	★★	★★
Snowshoe	★★★	★	★★★	★★★
Sokoke	★★★	★	★★	★★★
Somali	★★★	★★★	★★★	★★
Sphynx	★★★	★★	★★	★★
Tonkinese	★★★	★	★★★	★★★
Toyger	★★★	★	★★	★★★
Turkish Angora	★★★	★★	★★★	★★★
Turkish Van	★★★	★★	★★	★★★
Wild Abyssinian	★★★	★	★★	★★
Domestic Shorthair	★★★	★	★★★	✪
Domestic Longhair	★★★	★★	★★	★★

Glossary

Autosomal recessive mutation a mutation associated with the autosomes, which are the chromosomes present in the cell nucleus, aside from the sex chromosomes. Pairing a cat displaying a mutation of this type to a normal individual will result in cats that resemble this parent. When two such individuals carrying the recessive mutation mate, however, the likelihood is that some of their kittens will display this recessive trait.

Barring the darker, randomly distributed markings present on the legs of many tabby cats.

Bicolor a cat displaying areas of both white and colored fur, such as black and white or red and white. In the case of purebred cats, judging standards specify the relative distribution of these areas in the coat.

Blaze the area of fur, usually white, running down between the eyes and broadening out over the lips.

Bloodline the ancestry of a particular cat extending back over several generations—typically, but not exclusively, applied to purebred individuals.

Blotched areas of color linked with the classic form of tabby patterning that result in large patches, in the form of blotches, corresponding to the darker marking being apparent on the flanks.

Blue point one of the traditional **colorpoint** varieties, where the points—the face, ears, legs, feet, and tail—are a typical bluish-gray color, although this coloration will not be evident at birth in cats displaying such markings.

Bobtail a tail that is naturally shorter than normal, being reduced to a bob that curls downward. This characteristic is common in parts of Asia, being a feature of the Japanese and Kurelian bobtails. It is also apparent in breeds elsewhere, such as the Pixiebob and American Bobtail, as well as in the Wild Bobcat (*Lynx rufus*).

Break change in angle of the facial profile, typically from the head to the nose.

Breed a group of cats that have recognizably distinct characteristics, which are passed on to their kittens when they mate, thereby confirming that they **breed true**.

Breeding program a planned series of matings, undertaken by exhibitors with the aim of improving the quality of their stock, or as a means by which it is intended to establish a new breed.

Breed true the way that a cat produces offspring corresponding in actual appearance (although not necessarily color or patterning) to that of herself and her mate.

Brindling the intermingling of hairs of a different color; frowned on in the case of bicolor show cats but relatively common in nonpedigree individuals.

Broken point coloration this condition occurs in a **colorpoint** when the typical point color is broken, often by white fur, rather than being consistent over that part of the body.

Brush the description given to the tail, typically of semi-longhaired breeds, which is covered in long fur, even though the coat on the body may be quite short.

Bunny hopping the very distinctive gait seen in Manx and Cymric cats, associated with their long back legs, which resemble those of a rabbit.

Calico the term more commonly used in North America for **tortoiseshell**-and-white patterning. There are a number of different varieties, such as the dilute calico, which is white combined with blue and cream.

Chamois a type of leather, typically used for polishing—or as far as cats are concerned, for wiping the coat to create an attractive shine.

Chromosomal relating to the chromosomes, on which the **genes** are located. Chromosomes normally occur in pairs, within the nucleus of each living cell. Kittens obtain one set of chromosomes from each parent.

Classic description of tabby patterning, also known as the blotched tabby, due to the prominent blotches of darker color on the flanks, which are said to resemble oysters in shape.

Cobby a relatively stocky body shape that is quite thickset.

Colorpoint cats that can be distinguished by having darker areas of fur on their **points**. Typical examples include the Siamese and Himalayan breeds.

Compact short-bodied, compared with the rangy, elongated appearance of breeds such as the Siamese.

Convergent evolution similarities in appearance that develop as a result of external forces in different, unrelated breeds or species.

Crossbreeding the mating of two different breeds.

Dilute varieties the paler varieties of colors, with typical examples being blue being the dilute form of black; lilac in the case of chocolate; cream in the case of red.

DNA the genetic material— deoxyribonucleic acid—that encodes all the features of the organism, and serves as the genetic blueprint.

Dominant mutation a mutation that is characterized by the fact that if a cat of this type is paired with a normal cat, then a percentage of the offspring in the first generation should resemble the dominant characteristic. This makes it much easier to establish such mutations, compared with **recessive** ones.

Ear tuft the long lengths of hair present on the tips of the ears; associated with some breeds, such as the Abyssinian, which resemble those of some wild cats.

Enzyme a chemical in the body that impacts on a chemical reaction, with those in the digestive tract tending to be of most significance in cats.

Exotic (i) literally a foreign breed of cat and also (ii) a specific breed developed originally in North America from American Shorthairs crossed with Persians. Similar cats have been created using other shorthaired breeds.

F1, F2, F3, F4 the number of generations extending from a particular cross. Of particular significance both in terms of temperament and fertility in the case of wild cat-domestic cat crosses. The higher the number, the further the cats in question are removed from the original pairing.

F1 crosses the F here means "filial generation." In cats, this is the first cross, typically describing the kittens born from a mating between a wild cat and a domestic cat.

Feline Leukemia Virus (FeLV) a deadly infection striking the cat's immune system, for which there is no treatment. Can be spread via saliva through bites and also through nasal secretions. Vaccination is the only way to protect against it.

Feral a population of cats that had domestic ancestors, but have reverted to a free-living existence and are very wary of people.

Fertile the ability to breed successfully.

Folds a description either relating to (i) the **jowls**; (ii) the wrinkled areas of skin seen on the body of some hairless breeds such as the Sphynx; or (iii) a general description for Scottish Folds, which are distinguished by their folded ears.

Fur ball shed hairs, that stick to the rough surface of the cat's tongue when it is grooming itself, are swallowed, and end up coalescing in the stomach to form a pad. Regular grooming will help prevent this problem, which is most common in longhairs.

Furnishings the areas of hair that are evident within the ears of cats.

Gender the biological sex of a cat. Males are called toms, and females are queens.

Gene the basis for the transference of characteristics from one generation to another, via **DNA**. Genes are located on structures called **chromosomes**.

Genetic relating to genes, often in the context of a genetic weakness.

Gloves the white area of fur associated with some cats, such as Birmans, covering their front paws.

Grooming the process of keeping the coat in good condition and preventing the fur from becoming matted.

Guard hairs the longer, coarser outer fur in a cat's coat.

Heterochromia a difference in color between an individual's eyes; typically associated with white-coated cats that may have one blue eye and another of a different color.

Hybrid the mating of two different species, as typified by wild cat-domestic cat crosses.

Hypoallergenic less likely to cause an allergic reaction than normal. Some breeds such as the Russian are reputed to fall into this category.

Implant either (i) the process whereby feline embryos establish a connection with the wall of the uterus, before a placental link is created, or (ii) the process of inserting a microchip for identification purposes under the skin at the back of the cat's neck.

Inbreeding the mating together of closely related cats, typically mother-son or father-daughter, usually for the purpose of reinforcing a particular characteristic.

Induced ovulators a relatively unusual method of breeding, whereby the female does not have a set ovulatory cycle, but releases her ova in response to mating, increasing the likelihood of successful fertilization. Seen especially in relatively solitary animals, such as cats.

Jowls the enlarged folds of skin surrounding the chins of males of some breeds, such as British Shorthairs.

Kibble the name given to pieces of dry cat food.

Kinked used in the case of cats usually to describe the appearance of the tail that may not be straight, either for genetic reasons (typically in Siamese) or as the result of injury.

Laxative a substance used to increase mobility within the digestive tract, in cases of obstruction. Can be used in cats for treating constipation or for **fur balls**.

Litter term used to describe a group of kittens born to a female cat.

Longhair a means of dividing cats, on the basis of their coat length, distinguishing them from shorthaired cats. Some breeds such as the Munchkin occur in both forms.

Longies a description applied to both Manx and Cymric cats that have full-length tails.

Mackerel terminology used for tabbies that have a pattern of stripes resembling the skeleton of a fish extending down the sides of their bodies.

Marbled a patterning closely associated with the Bengal breed, as the result of the introducion of classic tabby patterning, resulting in a marbled effect.

Marking any darker or contrasting color on the coat, usually in the form of lines, bars, or spots.

Mascara lines the darker areas that extend back from the corners of the eyes in tabby cats.

Mating the act of reproduction.

Matted/matting entanglements in the coat, causing it to feel flat.

Melanin black pigment seen in the coat of many cats.

Mitted the pattern of white fur covering the front paws, being more extensive on the hind paws and feet. One of the three patterns that is recognized in Ragdoll cats.

Molt the process of shedding hair from the coat, which becomes more profuse in the spring.

Mutation a change in the genetic make-up associated with a particular characteristic such as shape of the ears or the length of the legs.

Muzzle the area at the front of the face, including the jaws.

Neuter prevent from breeding, usually by surgical means. Sometimes also described as altering.

Obesity excessive weight gain.

Odd-eyed the eyes are of different colors. See also **Heterochromia**.

Orthopedic relating to the skeleton, as in orthopedic surgery.

Outcross the use of unrelated cats in a breeding program.

Pads may refer to (i) the underside of the paws, which are free from hair, or (ii) the areas at the very base of individual whiskers.

Parasites organisms that live in or on the cat's body.

Peach fuzz term used to describe the very short, fine fur present on the body of the Sphynx, resembling the appearance of the skin of a peach.

Pedigree a cat that has a documented individual ancestry extending back over several generations.

Pet type a description used for a purebred cat that is not suitable for showing, possibly because of a flaw such as poor patterning or coloration.

Pixie cat a term that is applied to the Devon Rex, because the shape of its face and ears looks like those of a pixie, a mythological creature linked with the English county of Devon.

Points the extremities of the body, covering the face, ears, legs, feet, and tail. These distinguish a **colorpoint** breed, of which the Siamese is probably the best-known form.

Purebred a kitten (or older cat) that belongs to a distinctive breed.

Queen a female cat.

Recessive a genetic term, which means that when a cat displaying a recessive trait is mated with a normal individual, all the kittens will resemble normals. Only when two cats carrying the recessive trait mate is this feature then likely to become apparent in their offspring.

Rexing distinctive curly, wavy pattern of the coat associated with various breeds such as the Cornish and Selkirk rexes.

Ruff the longer fur seen around the neck of longhaired breeds such as the Maine Coon over the winter period, when their coat overall will be more profuse because of the cold.

Rumpies a term used for Manx and Cymric cats that lack tails.

Screening a means of detecting genetic abnormalities in DNA or through actual illness, through various veterinary procedures.

Seal point the darkest shade associated with colorpoint breeds.

Selective breeding describes breeding controlling the **mating** process, thereby determining which cats will breed together.

Self-colored a term used to describe a cat of a **solid** (single) color, such as a black or cream individual.

Sepia agouti a color variety associated with the Singapura breed, where there is dark brown ticking on the individual hairs, set against a contrasting warm, old ivory ground. Light and dark bands are separated, with the tips of the hairs being dark and the bases light.

Shaded dark tipping extending some distance down from the tips of light-colored hairs, creating a distinctive contrast in the coat, with the dark areas being more pronounced than in Chinchillas.

Smokes cats that display an even transformation in color along the hairs from light to dark, moving from their bases to their tips.

Solid-colored a cat that has a pure-colored coat, free from markings or patches of other color. See **self-colored**.

Sparkling coat a coat that glitters because of the contrast in the fur, resulting from banding, which causes differences in coloration along the length of the individual hairs.

Spontaneous mutation a mutation that crops up unexpectedly, as typified by the American Curl or Munchkin.

Spotted a form of tabby patterning that is especially characteristic of certain breeds, such as the Egyptian Mau.

Spraying the way in which male cats use their urine to scent mark their territory and warn off other cats.

Sterile a cat that is unable to reproduce.

Stray a cat that has left its home, or may have no home but has previously lived as a pet (as distinct from a **feral** cat).

Stumpies members of the Manx and Cymric breeds that do have some evident length of tail but not a full-length tail.

Tabby the most common type of patterning seen in cats. Irrespective of the markings, all tabbies have the outline of an M-shaped marking on their forehead.

Tear staining tear fluid that flows out of the eyes, rather than down through the tear ducts into the nose, because of a blockage. A problem encountered especially in Persian Longhairs.

Testes the area of the body where spermatozoa are stored, being evident below the tail as swellings in mature tom cats that have not been neutered.

Third eyelid the membrane usually concealed at the corner of each eye, which protrudes over the surface in cases of protracted illness in particular, where body condition has been lost.

Ticked/ticking alternating light and dark banding running down individual hairs in the coat.

Tipped the darker tips present on individual hairs in the coats of some cats. See **shaded**.

Tom term used to describe a male cat.

Torbie the description favored in North America to describe tortoiseshell tabbies.

Tortoiseshell a cat that traditionally appears to have cream, red, and black coloration in the coat, but many other tortoiseshell forms exist, both in **purebred** and ordinary domestic cats. For **genetic** reasons, tortoiseshells are almost invariably female, and males that do occur are likely to be sterile.

Ultra bald a cat without any hair at all, as typified by the Peterbald.

Undercoat the shorter, insulating layer of downy fur that there is in the coat of many breeds, especially those from northern climes.

Underparts the underside of the cat's body.

Vaccination a means of protecting cats from major killer diseases, by encouraging their body's own immune system to develop immunity.

Variant a form different from the normal.

Velour a means of describing a coat that has a plush texture.

Veterinarian a trained professional who helps prevent and also treats illnesses in cats and other animals.

Vocalizations vocal noises made by cats.

Walk to heel the way in which a cat—or, more commonly, a dog—walks on a harness and leash when exercising, just behind its owner, having been trained to act in this way.

Wean to start to take solid food (as distinct from mother's milk).

Wirehaired the wiry coat texture that is associated with the American Wirehair breed.

Zoologist a person who studies animals, their behavior, and their world. A zoologist is also concerned with conservation.

Further Resources

Further Reading

Alderton, David. *Wild Cats of the World.* Facts on File, 2003.

Alderton, David. *Cat Interpreter.* Readers Digest, 2006.

Alderton, David. *Cats (Smithsonian Handbooks).* Dorling Kindersley, 2010.

Collier, Marjorie. *Siamese Cats: A Complete Pet Owner's Manual.* Barron's Educational Series, 2006.

Davis, Karen Leigh. *The Exotic Shorthair Cat: A Complete Pet Owner's Manual.* Barron's Educational Series, 1997.

Geyer, Georgie Anne. *When Cats Reigned Like Kings: On The Trail of the Sacred Cats.* Andrews McMeel Publishing, 2004.

Helgren, J. Anne. *Abyssinian Cats: A Complete Pet Owner's Manual.* Barron's Educational Series, 1995.

Helgren, J. Anne. *Encyclopedia of Cat Breeds.* Barron's Educational Series, 1997.

Hornidge, Marilis. *That Yankee Cat: The Maine Coon.* Tilbury House Publishers, 2002.

Lauder, Phyllis. *The British, European and American Shorthair Cat.* Batsford, 1981.

Miller, Lynn. *The Guide to Owning an Oriental Shorthair Cat.* TFH Publications, 2000.

Morgan, Diane. *The Sneeze-free Cat Owner: Allergy Management & Breed Selection.* TFH Publications, 2007.

Morris, Desmond. *Cat Breeds of the World.* Viking Adult, 1999.

Pocock, Robine. *The Burmese Cat.* David & Charles, 1980.

Rice, Dan. *Bengal Cats: A Complete Pet Owner's Manual.* Barron's Educational Series, 2005.

Simonnet, Jean. *Chartreux Cat.* Auerbach Publishers, 1990.

Thompson, Will, and Eric Wichkam-Ruffle. *The Complete Persian.* Ringpress Books, 2002.

Urcia, Ingeborg. *The Russian Blue Cat.* Elias Holl Press, 1992.

Vousden, Linda. *Tonkinese Cats.* TFH Publications, 1998.

Major breed registries in North America

American Cat Fanciers' Association
P.O. Box 1949, Nixa,
MO 65714-1949, U.S.A.
www.acfacat.com

American Cat Association
8101 Katherine Avenue
Panorama City,
CA 91402, U.S.A.
No website at the time of compiling this book.

Canadian Cat Association
5045 Orbitor Drive,
Building 12, Suite 102
Mississauga, Ontario,
L4W 4Y4, Canada.
www.cca-afc.com

Cat Fanciers' Federation, Inc.
P.O. Box 661, Gratis,
OH 45330, U.S.A.
www.cffinc.org/

The Cat Fanciers' Association, Inc.
1805 Atlantic Avenue
Manasquan,
NJ 08736, U.S.A.
www.cfa.org/client/home.aspx

International bodies

Fédération Internationale Féline (FIFe).
Contact the national representative in your country, who can be found via the FIFe website.
http://fifeweb.org/wp/org/org_mem.php

The International Cat Association, Inc.
P.O. Box 2684
Harlingen,
TX 78551,
U.S.A.
http://www.tica.org

The Traditional Cat Association
18509 NE 279th Street
Battle Ground,
WA 98604, U.S.A.
http://traditionalcats.com/

World Cat Federation
Geisbergstrasse 2,
D-45139 Essen,
Germany
http://www.wcf-online.de/

Major breed registries in Europe, Africa, Asia, and Australia

Australian Cat Federation, Inc.
c/o Mrs. Nell Evans, Secretary,
P.O. Box 331, Port Adelaide BC,
AS 5015, Australia.
www.acf.asn.au

Cat Federation of South Africa
P.O. Box 4079, Vanderbijlpark
1900, Republic of South Africa
www.cfsa.co.za

Governing Council of the Cat Fancy
5 King's Castle Business Park,
The Drove, Somerset
TA6 4AG, U.K.
www.gccfcats.org

Hong Kong Cat Lovers' Society
Kowloon Central,
P.O. Box 70108, Hong Kong
www.hkcls.com

National Cat Club
c/o Dr. Phillipa Holmes,
Membership Secretary,
42 Jameson Road,
Bexhill-on-Sea, East Sussex,
TN40 1EJ, UK.
www.nationalcatclub.co.uk

New Zealand Cat Fancy, Inc.
Private Bag 6103,
Hawkes Bay Mail Centre,
Napier 4142, New Zealand
www.nzcatfancy.gen.nz

Singapore Cat Club
Orchard, P.O. Box 315,
Singapore 912399
www.singaporecatclub.com

Index

Acknowledgments

Marshall Editions would like to thank the following for their kind permission to reproduce their images.

Key: t = top **b** = bottom **c** = center **r** = right **l** = left

Front cover: Shutterstock/ Alex Staroseltsev **back cover**: Shutterstock/ Utekhina Anna

Pages: 1 Warren Photographic/ Tetsu Yamazaki; **2–3** Warren Photographic/ Mark Taylor; **4** Warren Photographic/ Jane Burton; **6** Warren Photographic/ Jane Burton; **8** Warren Photographic;/Mark Taylor; **9** Shutterstock; **10** Shutterstock; **11t** Shutterstock; **11b** Warren Photographic/ Jane Burton; **12** Warren Photographic/ Jane Burton; **13** Shutterstock; **13b** Warren Photographic/Mark Taylor; **14** Warren Photographic/Mark Taylor; **15** Warren Photographic/Mark Taylor; **16** Warren Photographic/Mark Taylor; **17** Warren Photographic/Mark Taylor; **18-19** Warren Photographic/Mark Taylor; **20** Warren Photographic/ Jane Burton; **21** Animal Photography/ Alan Robinson; **22** Shutterstock; **23** Animal Photography/ Alan Robinson; **24** Warren Photographic/ Jane Burton; **25** Animal Photography/ Alan Robinson; **26** Animal Photography/ Alan Robinson; **27** Animal Photography/ Alan Robinson; **28** Animal Photography/ Sally-Anne Thompson; **29** Animal Photography/ Alan Robinson; **30-31** Warren Photographic/Jane Burton; **32** Warren Photographic/ Jane Burton; **33** Warren Photographic/ Jane Burton; **34** Warren Photographic/ Jane Burton; **35** Animal Photography/Tetsu Yamazaki; **36** Animal Photography/Tetsu Yamazaki; **37** Warren Photographic/ Jane Burton; **38** Shutterstock; **39** Animal Photography/ Sally-Anne Thompson; **40** Animal Photography/ Alan Robinson; **41** Animal Photography/ Alan Robinson; **42t** Animal Photography/Alan Robinson; **42–43** Warren Photographic/Mark Taylor; **44** Animal Photography/ Tetsu Yamazaki; **45** Animal Photography/ Alan Robinson; **46** Shutterstock; **47** Animal Photography/ Tetsu Yamazaki; **48** Alamy/ Andrew Tiley; **49** Americanringtail.com; **50** Animal Photography/ Tetsu Yamazaki; **51** Shutterstock; **52** Animal Photography/ Tetsu Yamazaki; **53** Shutterstock; **54** Warren Photographic/Jane Burton; **55** Animal Photography/ Vidar Skauen; **56** Animal Photography/ Tetsu Yamazaki; **57** Warren Photographic/ Jane Burton; **58** DK Images/Marc Henrie; **59** Animal Photography/ Tetsu Yamazaki; **60** Animal Photography/ Tetsu Yamazaki; **61** Animal Photography/ Tetsu Yamazaki; **62** Animal Photography/ Tetsu Yamazaki; **63** Animal Photography/ Vidar Skauen; **64** Animal Photography/ Tetsu Yamazaki; **65** Animal Photography/ Tetsu Yamazaki; **66** Warren Photographic/Jane Burton; **67** Animal Photography/ Tetsu Yamazaki; **68** Animal Photography/ Tetsu Yamazaki; **69** Animal Photography/ Tetsu Yamazaki ; **70** Animal Photography/ Alan Robinson; **71** Animal Photography/ Tetsu Yamazaki; **72** Animal Photography/ Tetsu Yamazaki; **73** Animal Photography/Alan Robinson; **74** Animal Photography/ Tetsu Yamazaki; **75** Animal Photography/ Tetsu Yamazaki; **76** Animal Photography/ Tetsu Yamazaki; **77** Shutterstock; **78** Shutterstock; **79** Animal Photography; **80** Animal Photography/ Helmi Flick; **81** Animal Photography/ Helmi Flick; **82** Shutterstock; **83** www.PurringAngelsCattery.com **84** Elfcats.com/Karen Nelson; **85** Animal Photography/ Helmi Flick; **86** Shutterstock; **87** Animal Photography/ Helmi Flick; **88** Animal Photography/ Alan Robinson; **89** Animal Photography/ Helmi Flick; **90t** Getty Images/Cultura/Howard Kingsnorth; **90b** Getty Images/The Image Bank/ Yasuhide Fumoto; **91** Corbis/Ocean; **92** Graham Meadows; **93** Shutterstock; **94l** Animal Photography/Tetsu Yamazaki; **94r** Animal Photography/ Tetsu Yamazaki; **95** Animal Photography/ Tetsu Yamazaki; **96** Animal Photography/ Alan Robinson; **97** Animal Photography/ Tetsu Yamazaki; **98** Shutterstock; **99** Animal Photography/ Alan Robinson; **100** Animal Photography/ Tetsu Yamazaki; **101** Shutterstock; **102l** Animal Photogaphy/ Tetsu Yamazaki; **102r** Animal Photography/ Tetsu Yamazaki; **103** Animal Photography/ Tetsu Yamazaki; **104** Animal Photography/ Tetsu Yamazaki; **105** Ardea/ J.M. Labat; **106** Animal Photography/ Tetsu Yamazaki; **107** Animal Photography/ Tetsu Yamazaki; **108** Animal Photography/ Alan Robinson; **109** Animal Photography/ Alan Robinson; **110** Animal Photography/ Tetsu Yamazaki; **111** Animal Photography/ Helmi Flick; **112** Animal Photography/ Tetsu Yamazaki; **113** Ardea/ J.M. Labat; **114** Animal Photography/ Tetsu Yamazaki; **115** Animal Photography/ Tetsu Yamazaki; **116** Corbis/Reuters/Mike Blake; **117** Animal Photography/ Tetsu Yamazaki; **118** Ardea/ J.M. Labat; **119** Ardea/ J.M. Labat; **120** Animal Photography/ Tetsu Yamazaki; **121** Animal Photography/ Tetsu Yamazaki; **122** Animal Photography/ Tetsu Yamazaki; **123** Wind Haven Exotics/Carol Drymon; **124** Animal Photography/ Tetsu Yamazaki; **125** Animal Photography/ Tetsu Yamazaki; **126** Shutterstock; **127** Animal Photography; **128** Animal Photography/ Alan Robinson; **129** Animal Photography/ Tetsu Yamazaki; **130** Animal Photography/ Alan Robinson; **131** Graham Meadows; **132** Animal Photography/ Tetsu Yamazaki; **133** Animal Photography/ Alan Robinson; **134** Animal Photography/ Tetsu Yamazaki; **135** Animal Photography/ Tetsu Yamazaki; **136** Warren Photographic/ Jane Burton; **137** Warren Photographic/ Jane Burton; **138** Shutterstock; **140** Ardea/ J.M. Labat; **141** Animal Photography/ Helmi Flick; **142** Animal Photography/ Helmi Flick; **143** Shutterstock; **144** Shutterstock; **145** Animal Photography/ Tetsu Yamazaki; **146** Animal Photography/ Helmi Flick; **147** Animal Photography/ Vidar Skauen; **148** Shutterstock; **149** Animal Photography/ Tetsu Yamazaki; **150l** Warren Photographic/Mark Taylor; **150c** Warren Photographic/Jane Burton; **151** Warren Photographic/Mark Taylor; **152** Shutterstock; **153** Shutterstock; **154** Shutterstock; **155** iStock; **156** Warren Photographic/ Jane Burton; **157** Warren Photographic/ Mark Taylor; **158** iStock; **159** Shutterstock; **160** Shutterstock; **161** Shutterstock; **162** Shutterstock; **163** Shutterstock; **164** Warren Photographic/ Jane Burton; **167** Shutterstock.